"Don't invest in frontier and emerging markets until you read *The Culture Key*."

—Ghulam Destageer Haidari, Chief Sales Officer, Roshan Telecoms, Kabul, Afghanistan

"Over the course of thirty years of working with and alongside Americans as they try to develop business opportunities in other countries, I've found time and again that the biggest single factor separating successes from failures is an appreciation of the legal and cultural milieu in the target country. Nothing better prepares an international entrepreneur for success than a working knowledge of the ground rules of intercultural business, and nothing better provides that understanding than experience. Curt Laird clearly has that knowledge built on long experience, and he has the clarity of communication to share it all in a way easy to internalize and apply."

—Gregg Fairbrothers, founding director of the Dartmouth Entrepreneurial Network; president, Groups—Recover Together, Inc.; author of *From Idea to Success: The Dartmouth Entrepreneurial Network Guide for Start-Ups*

THE CULTURE KEY

SUCCESSFUL INVESTING AND ENTREPRENEURSHIP IN FRONTIER AND EMERGING MARKETS

CURT G. LAIRD

XANA Publishing

The Culture Key: Successful Investing and Entrepreneurship in Frontier and Emerging Markets

Curt G. Laird
Copyright © 2018 by Curt G. Laird
All Rights Reserved

Editors: Natalie Horbachevsky and David Sanford
Copyeditor: Janina Lawrence
Cover Design: Amjad Shahzad
Interior Design: Phillip Gessert

Published in the United States by Xana Publishing

ISBN: 978-1-7323500-0-7 (*paperback*)
ISBN: 978-1-7323500-1-4 (*hardcover*)
ISBN: 978-1-7323500-2-1 (*ebook*)
Version 1.0

DEDICATION

There is a richness in cross-cultural interactions that is often untapped. The beauty and depth in humankind's diversity is profound. I have found great personal growth in a lifetime of cross-cultural adventures in life and in business. I am grateful to all those diverse friends and family who have been a part of filling my life and work with the richness of relationship. Katrina, Dad and Mom, Johnathan, and Destageer, this book is a testament to your love and patience, and to the belief that business done well and done right has the power to transform nations.

CONTENTS

INTRODUCTION

In the spring of 2006, I found myself in a small room in southern Afghanistan, surrounded by twelve majestically bearded and robe-clad elders from a district influenced by the Taliban. Some of the men in that room were Taliban sympathizers; others, more likely, were active supporters. And yet, at that moment, I was the safest American in all of Afghanistan.

I had something these tribal elders wanted: mobile phone service for their community of business leaders, teachers, and officials. I was the regional executive director of Roshan, the newest and best mobile phone company in Afghanistan. Beside me in that room sat Destageer, an Afghan who was my deputy and close friend.

When I entered the meeting room, the only foreigner and without bodyguards, I didn't come armed only with a business plan for introducing mobile phone service to this dangerous region in Helmand province. I brought with me an understanding of the culture—a knowledge, born of experience and bolstered by Destageer's presence, to wend my way through a potentially tricky and possibly perilous negotiation with these elders from the towns of Sangin and Musa Qala.

The first question the elders asked me was, "Where are you from?" Fifteen fierce-looking Afghans in front of me were waiting intently for my answer. My mind raced as I contemplated telling them the truth about my American heritage.

Thankfully, I knew an important word: Pashtunwali.

The Pashtun tribe of Afghanistan is considered one of the fiercest warrior tribes and the most loyal to their code, known as Pashtunwali. Those who abide by that code believe the protection of guests is paramount—and guests like me were to be protected by their hosts, even with their lives. Relying on what I understood of this code, I swallowed hard and told them I was American. They nodded their heads in acknowledgement, and immediately asked, "So, when do we get mobile phone service?" It was down to business.

At Roshan, our biggest concern was protecting the safety and security of our engineers and maintenance techs, the people who installed antennas and kept them operating. I expressed this concern to the elders who, unsurprisingly, assured me that there would be no problem. But I needed to be absolutely sure.

Then I did something that called for every bit of faith I had in my understanding of their culture. I slammed my hand down on the desk and looked each elder sternly in the eye.

"You will never have mobile phone service if any one of my employees is even threatened!" I exclaimed. There was just a moment of stunned silence. I had no idea what went through their minds, but I hoped it was, "Boy, this American has balls!" Then all fifteen of the elders broke out in a simultaneous cacophony of absolute assurances that there was zero chance of problems. My risk had been rewarded.

A month later, we sent our four engineers to Helmand. They were met by a twenty-car convoy of these very elders, who escorted them north to their districts. They had called the American military; they had called the Taliban commanders; they had called their mothers to make it clear that our convoy was not to be disturbed. It was not, and our engineers returned safely to Kabul. The antenna we installed with the blessing of the elders became our highest revenue site within months, and led to many more. We could hardly keep up with the demand.

The author with a group of Afghan elders (not the elders referenced in the story above) (by Curt Laird)

As I sat sipping tea on that sweltering morning in southern Afghanistan, I bargained the success of our business—and indeed my life and that of my staff—on my understanding of the cultural code of Pashtunwali. The worldview of the Afghan elders with whom I was meeting was fundamentally different from my own in some very important ways. If I was to survive and succeed in business in this world, I had to learn to navigate these different waters effectively.

CALLING ALL COURAGEOUS INVESTORS AND ENTREPRENEURS

This book introduces courageous investors and entrepreneurs to the foundational skills and knowledge that are needed to find, build, and successfully manage thriving businesses in the world's most challenging economies.

In 2003, I joined a founding team of eight directors to start what would become a $1 billion mobile phone company in Afghanistan. In just three and a half years, Roshan turned an initial $40 million investment into over $200 million in annual revenue. The demand for our mobile phone service exceeded all expectations. Our business plan projected we would have 12,000 subscribers in six months; we had 12,000 in six days. Small riots broke out as Afghans swarmed the shops, desperate to obtain the means to connect to one another and to the world.

Every SIM card and airtime sale was conducted in the only viable currency at the time—U.S. dollars—and we soon had so much cash flowing in that we didn't know what to do with it all. There were no commercial banks able to secure the cash and no easy way to get it out of the country to pay equipment vendors. I had purchased three safes in Dubai, but they were overflowing within the first weeks. We resorted to stuffing wads of cash into our coats and transporting it to multiple residences around the city simply to spread our risk.

What was the secret to Roshan's success? Taking advantage of an extraordinary business opportunity was undoubtedly a big part of it. Until that moment, most people had to travel to neighboring Pakistan to make international calls. Now, mothers in remote villages could call their sons working in Dubai and businesspeople across Afghanistan could connect with markets for their products.

The success of Roshan was, however, not just about opportunity. It was also the result of hundreds of deals carefully brokered over cups of tea and thousands of moments in which we had to balance the ambition of entrepreneurship with navigating the labyrinth of mindsets hewn out of years of poverty and conflict.

If you are interested in investing in or building businesses in frontier and emerging markets, know this: the foundation of success in these endeavors is NOT entrepreneurial skills or experience. Nor is it simply finding opportunities; these markets are in many ways virgin markets. Business opportunities abound in such environments, from pharmaceuticals to commercial tailors, from frozen yogurt chains to food and beverage production and packaging. Rather, the real foundation of success in frontier and emerging markets is inter-cultural intelligence.

> The foundation of your success in frontier and emerging markets is inter-cultural intelligence!

For the purposes of this book, we will define inter-cultural intelligence as "a combination of the insights, competencies, attitudes, and behaviors that enable you to assess inter-cultural situations accurately, in order to engage effectively with the world around you."[1] Without inter-cultural intelligence, in-

---

1. Blankenburgh, Marco. "Inter-Cultural Intelligence." http://knowledge-workx.com/framework/inter-cultural-intelligence. Accessed February 22, 2018. The KnowledgeWorkx site also offers a different definition: "Why we use the term 'Inter-Cultural Intelligence'". KnowledgeWorkx. http://knowledgeworkx.com/articles/global-intelligence/366/why-we-use-the-term-inter-cultural-intelligence. Accessed December 12, 2017.

vestors and entrepreneurs cannot find long-term success in frontier markets.

There are overlapping definitions of frontier and emerging markets, with the former sometimes called a "pre-emerging" market. The principles in this book apply to the entire continuum, but going forward I will concentrate on frontier markets.

We will use the definition of a frontier market as a country that is relatively poor and early in its economic development, but "investable." It may or may not have a functioning equity or stock market, but has favorable foreign ownership laws and means to effectively repatriate profits when needed. Frontier markets carry inherent risk, but are usually primed to grow or "emerge."

Examples of frontier markets range from post-conflict countries like Afghanistan and Kurdistan/Iraq to countries like Lebanon, Nigeria, Pakistan, and Vietnam.

The challenge of structuring and managing successful deals in these environments is exacerbated by mindsets wrought by decades of conflict, poverty, or authoritarian rule. The evidence leaks out in protectionism, poor quality, the seeming inability to plan or unwillingness to take risks for the long-term. I draw mostly on experiences and stories from my time in Afghanistan to illustrate and explain these common mindsets. While most of these mindsets are intensified in conflict-affected environments, I have observed the same features at play in other countries as diverse as Egypt, Greece, Indonesia, Kenya, Nigeria, and Spain.

INVESTOR TIP

Cultural intelligence plays a critical role in every aspect of investing in frontier and emerging markets. Here are a few places in the process that demand inter-cultural intelligence:

Sourcing deals

- Understanding subtle characteristics of frontier markets that affect potential success. For instance:
  - Do "aspirational" products work in post-conflict frontier markets where the Survival Mindset remains strong?
  - How do you sell to women in conservative and poor-security markets?
- Identifying actual owners, especially unofficial, but powerful, owners who will never show up in any document (e.g., many female-owned businesses are effectively fronts for a husband/family/tribe)
- Identifying which businesses can fly "under the radar" to avoid negative intervention by corrupt authorities and powerful interests

Due diligence

- Getting "behind the veil" that hides so many things to outsiders
- Fully grasping that financial data is meant to enhance the honor, standing, or power of a company, not show its weaknesses
- Seeing that many businesses are more of a network of relationships than a set of processes and products

Recognizing and recruiting entrepreneurs

- Understanding what of the expected entrepreneurial

mindset and knowledge foundation is missing due to culture and recent country experiences

- Dealing with and mitigating the difficulty of extracting and revealing personal weaknesses or deficiencies of entrepreneurs in cultures where weakness is never shown

Ownership structures and dynamics

- Recognizing the dynamics and intricacies of family ownership
- Knowing how much to trust legal structures and documents
- Understanding the actual, as opposed to visible, decision-making process/hierarchy within ownership

Financial management

- Transforming the mindsets that limit the perceived need for financial and inventory controls
- Building systems (and peer/community pressure) to hold powerful owners accountable for expenses and personal loans

Navigating corruption

- Understanding the difference between corruption and "facilitating payments"
- Learning how to deal with corrupt tax officials who may hold you "hostage" or blackmail you

These challenges and many more demand a new and clearer way to navigate culture and mindsets in frontier markets.

HARD-WON EXPERTISE

It's often said that experience is the best teacher. That's true—and if you can learn from others' experiences, not just your own, all the better.

This book is the culmination of over thirty years starting, building, and managing businesses across the globe, fourteen of which were spent building successful businesses in Afghanistan, one of the world's most challenging investment climates.

I enjoyed the privilege of an upbringing that trained me to navigate cultures almost instinctually. As the son of a pilot, I lived in Costa Rica, Ecuador, the United States, Papua (formerly Irian Jaya, part of Indonesia), and Malaysia before I graduated from high school.

After earning my undergraduate degree in electrical engineering, I was quickly deployed by an aerospace company to manage their complex relationships with clients around the world. I worked in twenty-three countries over five years.

In 2002, I moved to Afghanistan to help establish a nonprofit Internet hub for the relief and humanitarian organizations in the country. I arrived two months before the Taliban was finally ousted[2] and stayed for the next fourteen years. The adjustment was profound. I distinctly remember the first time I witnessed rockets landing in our Kabul neighborhood. Naïve to the dangers, I ran to the window after the first rocket landed to see if I could tell how close it had come. The next time I was in the middle of a firefight, I was safely ensconced in the basement.

---

2. The Taliban began to slowly re-emerge in subsequent years, after seeing that the U.S. had turned its attention to Iraq and that the Afghan government was slow to implement the reforms needed for real progress.

Having been at war since 1978, Afghans had seen everything stripped clean, from the copper wires of almost every telephone line in the country to the hopes and dreams of an entire generation, who had known nothing but conflict and despair. After the American coalition finished routing the Taliban in 2002, there was an almost giddy sense of hope and relief in the country—and almost nothing on which to build a new society. Most materials, technical know-how and management experience were from the Soviets' decade of occupation in the 1980s. Whole neighborhoods were flattened and the markets laid waste. It was not much to build on, but the challenge made for exciting days.

When I joined Roshan in 2003, there were just eight of us, but we shared a vision to create a world-class mobile phone system. And that we did. Roshan helped put mobile phones into the hands of more than 80 percent of the Afghan people. After three and a half years with the company, I turned over my position as executive director of regions to my Afghan deputy, Destageer, whom I had hired and mentored. It was time for me to get back to my passion for starting companies.

In 2008, I co-founded Silk Road Solutions, a leadership and business skills training company, with Susan Ryan, an experienced inter-cultural management professional with deep knowledge of Afghan culture. I had experienced firsthand the consequences of the ravages of war and poverty on business leadership skills at Roshan. In those consequences, we saw both a business opportunity and an opening for social development in the country. We worked with leaders in the private sector, non-governmental organizations, and the Afghan civil sector as they moved toward their vision for a new leadership mindset in Afghanistan.

Later, Destageer and I established a business accelerator, the Business Innovation Hub, at the American University in

Kabul. With U.S. government seed money and the support of Leslie Schweitzer, president of Friends of the American University of Afghanistan (FAUAF), we took everything learned at Roshan and Silk Road Solutions and engaged small and medium businesses in the pursuit of sustainable growth and profits.

Though I had already worked in dozens of countries, the Afghans and their country were my greatest training ground in cross-cultural entrepreneurship, investment, and ongoing management. The country is still one of the hardest frontier markets in the world. Every challenge is magnified and every success harder won. The daily, painful reality of over three decades of war and poverty has carved profound changes into the mindsets of its people. These mindsets are layered on top of a rich culture and thousands of years of history. They have, I confess, often been difficult for me to understand or to navigate.

Yet, against all odds, I succeeded. How?

Yes, I know a lot about mobile communications networks and entrepreneurship. More importantly, however, I know that emerging frontier economies, such as those rebuilding after war, provide some of the most profitable business opportunities. I'm not talking about profiting from the war itself; I am talking about rebuilding an entire country and all the opportunities that presents. Where there's high risk, there's high return.

I have learned through hard experience what it takes to *succeed* as a frontier market investor and cross-cultural entrepreneur. Better yet, I know how to *become* one and I can guide you toward that same goal. I use my experience to work with investors and entrepreneurs as they identify, invest in, and grow companies within these challenging markets.

This book distills the lessons I have learned to set the foundation for becoming a successful cross-cultural investor and entrepreneur. It is not intended to be an academic treatise that will sit on someone's shelf. Rather, I want to present a practical guide to those investing in, and building and managing businesses in emerging and frontier economies. My goal is to equip you with the tools to navigate the complex cultural dynamics of these frontier markets—and find success in employing these learnings in your life and business.

THEN:

My friend and colleague, Hafizi, standing in his destroyed home in Kabul in 2002 (by Curt Laird)

NOW:

In 2015, the same neighborhood is transformed to fit the huge influx of people to Kabul (© by Ton Koene/Alamy Stock Photo)

THEN:

Destruction (and budding business in the shadows) near my home in Kabul in 2002 (by Curt Laird)

NOW:

Safi Landmark Hotel and Kabul City Centre shopping mall in 2015 (Used with permission of Safi Landmark Hotel & Suites, Kabul, Afghanistan)

THEN:

In 2002, the entrepreneurs were working with very little, in this case an old hospital bed (by Curt Laird)

NOW:

In 2015, modern businesses full of products (© by ZUMA Press, Inc./Alamy Stock Photo)

INVESTOR TIP: BUSINESS OPPORTUNITIES IN FRONTIER MARKETS

There are large investment deals in frontier markets. I was on the founding team of a $40 million investment that was valued at $800 million by British banks three and a half years after inception. But these deals are high stakes games that need massive political influence and highly technical skillsets.

An investment space that is often missed is that of buying all or part of existing companies. The owners have a good product or service, but do not know how take it to the next level. In most cases what is needed is not rocket science at all. These businesses are in the sweet spot of manageable risk, strong returns, and social responsibility. They often have annual revenue of less than $1 million (at times less than $500K), but have the potential of being sector leaders and of reaching revenues of $5 million and above. Investing in a wide range and number of these companies spreads the risk and keeps you below the radar screen of the warlords and corrupt government officials.

At the Business Innovation Hub accelerator in Kabul we took on as clients a number of these businesses. A suit and uniform manufacturer, a commercial bakery, a frozen yogurt franchisee, and a pharmaceutical manufacturer are some examples. Each had reached the limit of their abilities to scale into relatively untapped markets. We began to implement basic, but essential changes (computerized accounting and basic financial analysis, outbound sales teams, asset, and inventory control, etc.). Some made the changes and pushed beyond their previous limits. Thirty percent growth in a matter of months was not uncommon. But others balked at making the difficult choices and went back to stagnation or slowly died off.

It was extremely frustrating to see these high-potential businesses wither away for want of a few basic changes. It felt like money left on the table. One of the strongest lessons we learned was that we could have been more successful if we had the leverage of an equity stake to make necessary changes. However, by the rules of the accelerator funding, we could not. We needed an investment fund to step in and, in most cases, take a majority stake at relatively little cost. Unfortunately, you could count on one hand the number of private investment funds in all of Afghanistan, and only one even dabbling in this space. It has untapped potential.

Why the need to take a majority stake? In many frontier markets, a minority stake in a company is not tenable. Minority ownership rights are not well-defined and mostly unenforceable. Majority ownership gives you the right to make the difficult, but necessary, changes. In countries where foreign majority ownership is not allowed, it is usually not impossible to creatively guard your minority stake and have enough leverage to mandate the necessary operational changes; however, it can be challenging.

We looked at hundreds of businesses in this sweet spot and came away more convinced than ever that a frontier market investment fund could have made excellent returns in this niche.

The investment funds which did attempt to enter the market—often with donor backing—rarely had the inter-cultural intelligence to succeed. They did not heed the lessons in this book and walked away having wasted millions of dollars and dashed the hopes of numerous entrepreneurs.

The time has come for a new, inter-culturally intelligent investment fund for frontier markets.

BEFORE WE DIVE IN

Every country is composed of a variety of people from many different cultures—no country is a mono-culture and every individual in that country has a spectrum of characteristics. However, sometimes one has to paint with a broad brush to make a point. In this book, when I write that a culture has this or that characteristic, it is meant to make the reader aware of that thread and see its varied degrees within every individual in that culture. It is not meant to imply that every individual has the same degree of that characteristic. As a result, the tools and frameworks I will introduce are generous and broad; they allow for people to fit in every corner. But primarily, they seek to give structure and descriptions to the prevailing culture and mindsets in order to form successful partnerships for everyone's benefit.

Let's begin the journey.

WHERE WE ARE GOING

This book is divided into four parts.

In Part I, I'll introduce an invaluable tool that will help you unlock an understanding of the behaviors you may witness in frontier and emerging markets. With this tool in mind, we'll discuss the attitude and posture that investors and entrepreneurs need to bring to their work in these markets around the world, and establish a framework to carry us forward in our work deciphering culture.

In Part II, we'll look at the worldviews predominant in many frontier and emerging markets and look at how this differs from the worldview held by most Western businesspeople.

We'll build on this work in Part III and delve deeper into cultural dimensions to understand how people in frontier and emerging markets think about relationships, communication, and productivity, among other key business issues.

Finally, in Part IV, we'll explore the mindsets of scarcity and survival that emerge as a result of societies' experiences, particularly traumatic ones.

Armed with these tools and insights, I am confident you can find success in cross-cultural contexts.

PART I
FRAMEWORK AND TOOL

CHAPTER 1

THE BELIEF TOOL

Where I grew up in Papua, there is a freshwater lake teeming with saltwater sharks. Centuries ago, the lake was a large bay of the sea. Then an earthquake caused a massive landslide that closed the inlet. Over many years, the newly formed lake became less and less salty as river water flowed in. The saltwater sharks inhabiting that former bay slowly adapted to their new environment. Had the change been sudden, they would have died. Now they would die if they were taken back to their native saltwater.

The sharks never knew that their water was changing. Just as a fish swims in its water and never sees it[3], we pay very little attention to the significance of the cultural context in which we are "swimming"—*until* we find ourselves, like freshwater sharks, suddenly plunged into the salty Pacific Ocean. The question then immediately becomes: Can I adapt?

---

3. This fish analogy was first applied to culture by Derek Sivers in an online article titled, *"Fish don't know they're in the water"*, https://sivers.org/fish, June 19, 2011.

Can I adapt?

Over the years, those first few minutes after stepping off a plane in a new land have become some of my favorites. The air-lock on the plane door is released and, stepping onto the jet-way, the first smells and sounds of this new place come rushing in. Exiting through those familiar airport immigration doors, the senses are overloaded with everything new and different. The humidity that hangs thick in the air, the sound and throng of taxis (both official and non) that clamber for your business, the unfamiliar language or accents. Everything new.

This first introduction to a new context is often over-whelming. These differences, however, are merely surface re-flections of far more fundamental differences that lie below. They only hint at what is beneath, the largest part of the mas-sive iceberg of understanding an unfamiliar culture.

Edward T. Hall, one of the founding fathers of inter-cul-tural communication studies, said, "Culture hides much more than it reveals, and strangely enough what it hides, it hides most effectively from its own participants."[4]

Even in marriage, these hidden differences surface fre-quently. As well as I think I know my wife, Katrina—who is British and Finnish—rarely a week goes by when I do not think, "Wow! She really thinks that way? It's so foreign to me." Her water is most definitely different from my own and, yes, sometimes we are both forced to ask the question, "Can I adapt?"

To adapt, we must first figure out what we are seeing. But what you see in any situation may be entirely different from

---

4. Hall, E. T. *The Silent Language*. Greenwich, CT: Fawcett, 1959.

what someone else sees, especially if they are from a different culture. Whose reality is the "truth"? What if both are true?

As part of my work, I run leadership training courses for frontier market leaders. At the beginning of every course, I hold up a sheet of paper—blank on one side and illustrated on the other. Holding the blank side towards the participants, I ask them what they see. A perplexed look descends across their faces. One or two may venture a response, "Nothing, the sheet is blank."

"What are you saying?" I reply, incredulous. "We are looking at the same thing! There are words and pictures on the paper; can't you see them?"

"No, it's blank," they reply, this time more confidently.

"Are you crazy?" I taunt them, trying to put on my most convincing act. "Are you blind?"

Invariably, some do not catch the act and rise to the defense of their view. When things are at a feverish pitch, I slowly turn the paper around, revealing what I have seen all along—an illustrated piece of paper. I stand back and watch as the light bulbs go on in their heads as they begin to understand that our views of reality can be diametrically opposed to one another—and yet both can be true.

The paper is the "Truth" with a capital "T"; each side is "truth" with a small "t." I see one side and they see the other. Would it not be helpful to catch a glimpse of how other cultures view their side of the paper? How can we presume to understand another individual, from another culture, without seeing life from their perspective and even questioning our own truths?

It is impossible to move forward in business without acknowledging this incongruity in cultural truths. But Western businesses rarely understand or acknowledge the full impact of culture on the decisions they make. Developed nations export assumptions that often kill success in frontier and emerging markets. While there are core investment and entrepreneurial truths and rules worldwide, understanding how these truths apply in other cultures is often overlooked or dealt with in a cursory manner. Yet, your degree of success in frontier and emerging markets largely depends on how well you deal with culture.

There are plenty of easy-to-find lists warning against certain actions when you enter another culture, a kind of cheat sheet to cross-cultural business. In Indonesia, for example, never give things with your "dirty" left hand and never show the bottoms of your "dirty" feet. In Japan, never put a newly received business card into the wallet that goes in your back pocket near your butt. In Nigeria, never look an elder directly in the eyes when you greet him or her. Never, never, never—the list goes on and on.

These lists are an important starting point for every new cross-cultural adventure. They often help you avoid immediately offending colleagues, business partners or clients. However, they will *never* be exhaustive or nuanced enough to help you navigate the complexities of a new business environment. There will come a day—often soon into your journey in a new country—when you face the inevitable situation that does not fit any of those rules you memorized.

Rather than simply memorizing a limited (and limiting) list of cultural dos and don'ts, you need a tool to help you identify, interpret, and respond to the underlying beliefs that drive decisions and behavior in your new environment. You need a lens that allows you to see any and every action or behavior and understand the belief that lies beneath it.

You need the Belief Tool.

The Belief Tool

The Belief Tool reveals profound insights into other cultures and, critically, enables you to identify responses that get you to your goals, whether investment goals, management goals, or simple personal goals in a new culture.

At the core of the Belief Tool are two assertions:

1. Every *action or behavior* comes from a core *belief*; and
2. A person's actions are always consistent with his or her beliefs.[5]

---

5. This is not counter to the concept of cognitive dissonance. Often there are conflicting beliefs. However, the resulting action or behavior reveals which of those beliefs is the consistently stronger of the two or it shows that "in this situation, X belief is stronger than Y belief."

At its most basic, beliefs are convictions we hold deeply, "a feeling of certainty about what something means."[6]

Our beliefs are at the center of all we feel and do. From them flow emotions and feelings, which in turn, drive actions and behaviors.

TWO BELIEFS MEET IN A DARK ALLEY

Imagine you're in a dark alley, when a man you do not know starts walking towards you, with one hand held behind his back. If you believe his hand holds a pistol, what emotions arise? Fear, almost certainly. From that emotion comes action—fight, flight, or freeze.

But what if you believe he is holding a dozen red roses or a gift behind his back? Your emotion is decidedly more positive: friendship, appreciation, romance, love? Your action is most likely to move toward him, not away.

See how your action was entirely dictated by your belief, even given the exact same situation?

The Belief Tool is powerful not simply because it helps you unpack the beliefs that drive another's behavior or decisions. It is powerful because it can reveal what lies at the root of cross-cultural conflicts and help you chart a way forward.

Cross-cultural conflicts arise most often when we respond to a behavior that conflicts with one of our core beliefs. That belief may seem so obvious or "essential" to the way that we understand the world that we rarely articulate it, even to ourselves. We assume that the objectionable behavior carries the same negative significance for our counterpart that it does for us. As a result, we confront the behavior in the way it "should"

---

6. Bennett, Ty. "The True Definition of Belief." Ty Bennett. August 4, 2009. Accessed December 12, 2017. http://tybennett.com/the-true-definition-of-belief/.

be confronted according to *our* belief system. Very often, this simply concludes with further offense and misunderstanding.

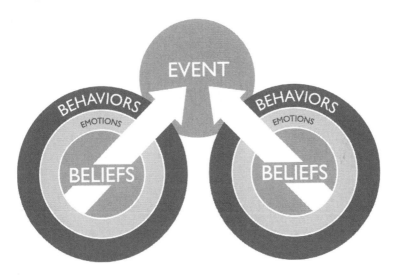

Let's look again at the example of the man walking down the dark alley with his hand behind his back (the "Event"). Consider the situation from the perspective (i.e., "Beliefs") of the man with the flowers or gift. If I'm that man, I am both crushed and confused; my intention is to present you with a token of my friendship and love and you scream and run away. My assumption is that you knew my intent. The reality, however, is that my impact on *you* is based on *your* belief, NOT on *my* intent.

My impact on you is based on
your belief,
NOT on my intent.

The same event causes different behaviors and emotions based on the belief of each person involved.

Use the Belief Tool as a lens to look through in every situation you encounter, whether it's discerning the negotiating tactic of the person sitting across from you on a critical deal, understanding the motivation and values of the entrepreneur you're planning to invest in, or confirming the veracity of some vital business information reported to you by a local employee. Used diligently, it will help you understand the behaviors you see and the decisions being made. More importantly, it will help you work out effective responses to any situation.

The Belief Tool is the core of this book and illustrates the book's central tenet:

Every human BEHAVIOR comes out of a core BELIEF.
And the central practice:

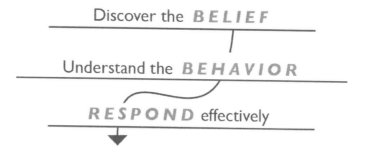

CHAPTER 2

NOT A WALK IN THE PARK: CURIOSITY AND HUMILITY

I was walking alone outside Kabul, quietly exploring the countryside, and minding my own business. Suddenly, I saw in front of me an urgent sign: "You're in a minefield, dummy!" (Okay, that's a paraphrase, but it's what the sign told me.)

I stood there with a drop of sweat beginning to form on my brow, pondering what my best next move would be. I turned my head and saw my fresh footprints in the dust behind me. Carefully I turned myself around and began the long walk back along those prints.

It felt like trying to walk on a six-inch-wide beam on top of the Empire State Building.

Interactions between people of different cultural backgrounds can be littered with mines, too—cultural land mines.

If you say or do the wrong thing to someone you want to do business with, you may find yourself blowing up potential opportunities.

Culture can be a minefield.
One misstep can be catastrophic.

When I was launching Roshan, I had to meet with Ismail Khan, the powerful warlord and governor of the western Afghan province of Herat. We were the new kid on the block in terms of mobile phone companies, and the only other system was partially owned by the very government he represented. He could have shut us down overtly or made life impossible. If I said the wrong thing, inadvertently acted in some way that dishonored him, or just used body language that didn't communicate respect, I would have triggered a cultural landmine. Because I knew how to approach the minefield, though, we walked out with his blessing.

To avoid cultural landmines and succeed in frontier markets, you need to take on a posture of curiosity and humility.

Succeeding in frontier markets
requires that you take on a
posture of curiosity and humility.

Western arrogance too often walks with its head held high, ignoring the signs—and blows itself to cultural smithereens. That is simply not good for business, any way you cut it.

The image of curious toddlers comes to mind; they are constant learners, unhindered by the curse of what they think they know. This is often an uncomfortable posture for entrepreneurs and businesspeople to assume, as projecting confidence has been a key to success in their native environments.

No matter how humble you and I may think we are, most of us remain remarkably committed throughout life to the belief that our experiences and interpretations of the world are valid, complete, and even the *right ones*. No other experience will more quickly and devastatingly shake that assurance than living, working, and managing cross-culturally.

KNOW *THAT* YOU DON'T KNOW

Blue burqas are among the most ubiquitous images of Afghanistan. Many Afghan women wear them to shield themselves from wondering (and wandering) eyes. Mothers gather their children like chicks around them, protecting them from the dust and mud thrown up from the street. In a gust of wind, you sometimes spot the flash of red sequined trousers, fishnet stockings or some other outlandish hidden style. In the big cities, black stiletto heels frequently peek out from under the folds of fabric.

These are not the only veils that make seeing and understanding people difficult in cultures different from our own. There is always a veil to the outsider. It may be gossamer or it may be opaque, but it is always there. You will never fully see behind the veil, unless you were born in the country and experienced its history. You can learn to see further behind the veil and do more with what you do see, but to succeed across the cultural divide, no principle is more important to understand than to first "know that you don't know."

For success cross-culturally, no
principle is more important than:
Know that you don't know.

The consequences of cultural arrogance can be devastating to businesses. Even seemingly small errors have the potential to cause enormous offense. They can completely derail an important business deal or destroy the loyalty of crucial employees.

In the early days of Roshan, Destageer and I met with a high-powered and high-priced European marketing consultant to review packaging mock-ups for a campaign geared toward selling mobile phones and service to Afghanistan's new generation.

The bright yellow packaging immediately caught my eye. I turned to Destageer, "Is this color okay? What would it signify to an Afghan?"

The look of alarm in his eyes told me everything before he spoke. "It's the color of rejection!" he exclaimed. "In important parts of this country, yellow is the color a woman wears if she is rejecting a suitor."

"It looks okay to me," the consultant said, waving dismissively.

I was shocked! Would you announce the birth of your first child with dark and somber colors? Of course not, it would be done with all things bright and vibrant[7]. The arrogance of the Western marketing "guru" in dismissing Afghan perception in favor of his own beliefs made me deeply angry, and I'm sure he did not miss my disgust. More than that, though, it was just bad business.

---

7. For more information on colors and culture, go to https://informationis-beautiful.net/visualizations/colours-in-cultures/.

At Destageer's insistence, we changed the yellow to orange and the campaign was a success. But I hoped that the consultant had learned a good lesson: to know that he didn't know everything about the culture within which he was operating.

KNOW *WHAT* YOU DON'T KNOW

We often do not know what questions to ask, even when we are curious.

How do we learn the right questions to ask and the most important signs to watch for? Where do we find the answers to those questions, once we have asked them?

You most likely know the answers to these questions in your own culture, but you need to acknowledge that you don't know the answers in other cultures.

Among the most important business-critical questions you cannot answer at the outset of operating in a frontier market are how to:

- recognize the subtleties of the consumer market in a new culture
- discern the authenticity and accuracy of reported numbers and information during due diligence
- close a deal
- identify the "influencers" and leverage the unique social fabric for viral marketing
- admonish an employee (and where and when)
- effectively communicate respect
- enter and greet a room where persons of varying social ranks sit and stand
- greet your employees each day
- increase loyalty among employees

- know when is the right time to micromanage
- demand quality and get it
- give a customer bad news
- hold a vendor accountable for a failure

These examples are only meant to show the complexity of *what you don't know;* there is no way you can memorize the answers to these questions before immersing yourself in another culture. This is where the Belief Tool and the framework we will expand on can play a critical role in navigating *what you don't know.*

"IS THIS BELIEF WORKING FOR YOU?"

When we discover, to our chagrin, that the assumptions and strategies that have made us successful within our own cultural context no longer work, we have one of two choices:

We can obstinately lock ourselves in to our own cultural beliefs and behaviors, insisting that the way we see it is the "right" way.

OR

We can engage in the hard and rewarding work of understanding and responding to the core beliefs of those within the new context.

Choosing the second option does not mean that we bend to every cultural belief. As you will see in this book, there are strategic moments when effective business leaders must challenge employees and teams to work counter to deeply engrained cultural behaviors that inhibit innovation and progress. In order to do this effectively, however, you must first understand the core beliefs that drive and determine those behaviors.

It is easy to get into right/wrong conversations about particular cultural beliefs, especially when we begin to operate in a new culture.

As we swim into different water, we often respond by saying that it is the water, not us, that should adapt. We complain, saying "This water is too salty!" or "This water doesn't have enough salt!" All the while we resist the need for our own attitudes and practices to adapt.

Resist the urge to draw quick judgments! Try swimming in their water; there may, in fact, be much to learn from the ways people in this new culture operate. Be aware that your cultural biases will get into the mix.

On the other hand, however, do not be afraid to make judgments. It would be dangerously naïve to suggest that any culture is entirely free of weaknesses in terms of doing business. It is *not* cultural arrogance to identify those weaknesses correctly and to mitigate them.

Ask the simple question,
"Is this belief working for you?"

Asking the simple question, "Is this belief working for you?" is far more effective than engaging in right/wrong discussions.

To put it differently, "Will this belief bring you to your vision?"

Afghanistan was just emerging from thirty years of protracted and violent conflict, severe Taliban oppression, and fierce ethnic strife, when I became part of the start-up management team at Roshan. Quality work was nowhere to be seen.

When we contracted builders to construct the brick and mortar walls around the antenna sites, we were happy when they finished roughly on time. A couple of weeks later, however, the walls began to crack and settle. The builders had sacrificed quality to finish quickly, save money, get paid, and buy food for their large families.

When confronted, they said, "We built the wall, you paid us, end of story." The prevailing attitude towards quality was infuriating to us, who were building a business that needed the antenna sites to last at least as long as its fifteen-year license. It was also understandable. Suggesting that Afghans invest in quality for the future simply didn't work, when they were just trying to survive in the present.

As an outsider, how do you deal with beliefs that limit effectiveness or actively hamper the ability of individuals or businesses to reach their vision? And how do you do this without coming across as a cultural imperialist? The seeming total disregard for quality may seem very wrong to you; it is likely entirely sensible, even right, to the locals. You will forever be fighting a losing battle, if you try to impose the quality standard without dealing with the underlying belief.

The only hope for changing unhelpful behaviors is to help people ask the question, "Is it working for me?"

A cost-benefit exercise can be a useful way to ask this question.

When we came across what seemed to be a limiting belief at any of our businesses in Afghanistan, we got out a big flip chart and did a cost-benefit exercise of that belief.

We might set out the belief that "Quality is *not* worth the time, money, and energy." The team then wrote down the benefits of not spending time, money, and energy on quality. For example, investments in quality are more expensive and more time consuming; tomorrow is not guaranteed in a time of conflict, so why waste the effort; it's hard to get people to implement quality; etc.

Next, we listed the costs of not valuing quality: things do not last; there is no pride of workmanship; it is more expensive in the long run; we have to keep redoing it over and over; it does not get us to our vision of a progressive nation; it does not call us to a higher, world standard; etc. We would usually run out of space on the costs side.

We would then stand back to look at our chart and everything we had recorded. Clearly, the beliefs about quality had worked throughout the years of conflict. However, they were not conducive to building an enduring mobile phone system, let alone a peaceful and stable country.

The Afghans themselves looked at the list and said, "The costs are too high! We *must* change our country's belief about quality and it needs to start here!"

There was no right/wrong discussion by a foreigner. There was no coercion to believe a certain way. There was no judgment or pressure.

The Afghans owned it and the awareness of this limiting belief became the first step of transformation. From that moment on, every time a choice about quality arose—even simple choices such as whether to buy the ubiquitous and cheap Chinese water heater or the well-built Korean model for a little more money—it was made with a new mindset born out of a new belief.

Shift the belief, shift the behavior.

As a Westerner used to Apple and Mercedes Benz quality, you can preach quality until you're blue in the face and get frustrated when it's not valued. The actions that come out of a limiting belief will never change, however, unless that belief is exposed and transformed.

This is the power of the Belief Tool. It helps us understand where our own actions come from. Furthermore, it exposes the beliefs that may be keeping us from the success we desire for ourselves and for those we are investing in.

One final story illustrates the different cultural waters we each swim in and how those beliefs can clash in the most unusual circumstances.

Notice anything unusual about the orientation of this toilet? (by Curt Laird)

We were renovating our Roshan office in Herat. The work was going well and it was time for me to have the international architect fly in from Kabul to give some more instructions, this time about the office's completely redesigned public toilets.

All was going well until he showed the position of the toilets in the narrow stalls. "No, no, no!" was the horrified response of the Afghans gathered. The tension in the air crackled. Now, I know toilets are a subject talked about with hesitancy in most cultures, but what was this all about? "You can't face the toilet that direction!" they cried in unison.

"What do you mean? There's only one direction it will fit in this narrow stall."

"It's an outrage!" they cried.

I knew there was a storm raging in the narrow confines of that ripped-out bathroom. I could visualize the headlines: American Dies in Afghanistan with Head in Toilet. With trepidation, I asked one of the most important cross-cultural questions: Why?

"It's offensive to have your front or rear facing Mecca!" I almost laughed, not because I disrespected their strictures, but because I was so poignantly reminded again of how easy it is to get tripped up in cross-cultural relations. The architect retreated to Kabul with one of the most powerful lessons: **know that you don't know.**

CHAPTER 3
A FRAMEWORK FOR UNDERSTANDING BELIEFS

An international business friend of mine shared the following story of a situation gone awry because of a difference in belief systems.[8]

A Kuwaiti company hired a South African to manage their partnership with a Dutch manufacturing firm, which was failing to comply with the specifications determined by their contract.

For months, the Kuwaiti owner had tried without success to resolve the problem. When the South African manager of-

---

8. This story was shared with me by my friend, Marco Blankenburgh, international director of KnowledgeWorkx in Dubai, who also wrote about his experience on his website: http://knowledgeworkx.com/articles/global-intelligence/361/the-three-colors-of-worldview-in-conflict-resolution

fered to help, saying, "I've got a bit of Dutch blood in me", the owner gladly agreed.

The Kuwaiti owner organized for a delegation of the Dutch company to visit Kuwait, and permitted his South African manager to lead the meeting so that the issues could be discussed and resolved in a "Dutch manner." As he observed the meeting's proceedings, the Kuwaiti became increasingly uncomfortable.

The South African manager entered negotiations confidently and directly. He placed the contract in the center of the table and declared, "Here are the issues. These are the ways you have not been compliant. We need to deal with this!" As discussion became more heated, the South African pressed on firmly, at times even being harsh in order to set the record straight. At the end of the meeting, he succeeded in getting a better response from the Dutch than the company had expected.

The South African manager was elated at the success of the meeting. But his Kuwaiti boss was horrified. A week later the South African was called into his boss's office and fired.

The direct approach to negotiation, which had been so successful with the Dutch delegation, violated deeply held values of the Kuwaiti owner. The South African manager and his Dutch counterparts shared a belief that conflicts should be resolved on the basis of legal and contractual "facts." In the eyes of the Kuwaiti owner, however, the failure to show hospitality and the direct nature of negotiation had completely undermined relational capital that he had worked for years to cultivate. Indeed, it was the emphasis on a relational, honor-maintaining communication style that had failed to get the Kuwaiti company a solution.

A COMMON LANGUAGE AND
FRAMEWORK TO UNDERSTAND BELIEFS

The consequences of not understanding the cultural beliefs of people in frontier markets can be catastrophic for the success of both your business and your professional prospects. Conversely, the ability to understand and navigate these cultural dynamics can and will be your key differentiator.

> The ability to understand and navigate cultural dynamics is the key differentiator that sets you apart.

Like sailors who must understand what lies below the surface of the water to set a safe course for their vessel, investors, entrepreneurs, and business managers must set their course with an understanding of the vast array of beliefs and attitudes that lie below the surface of their daily interactions. Your success in doing business cross-culturally depends in large part on recognizing and working with those differences.

But how to start? When it all looks and feels so foreign, it is useful to be able to describe a particular culture with some sort of common language. A description allows you to more objectively look at a culture, or a situation within a culture, and understand more fully the dynamics present.

In the pages that follow, I will begin to set out that common language or framework by describing three *worldviews*—collections or bundles of beliefs that tend to exhibit themselves together in specific cultures. We will then delve deeper into the bundles of beliefs that make up worldviews by introducing *cultural dimensions*. Finally, we will look beyond inherited cultural beliefs and explore the *mindsets* that emerge as a result of societies' experiences, particularly those of conflict or instability, chronic poverty, or political oppression.

See the behavior,
dig for the belief.

Remember, every behavior or action you see while navigating a culture flows out of a core belief. Discover the belief and you will not only understand better how to interpret the behavior, but you will also be able to craft an effective response. Your success in business in frontier markets depends on it.

INVESTOR TIP

There is often an assumption that members of the diaspora understand the local culture, despite having spent years away during which significant events and changes took place. Second-generation children of immigrant families, returning to their parents' homeland, may similarly fail to realize the ways in which they are more in sync with their passport culture than that of their parents. This can lead to disastrous investments and programs born out of arrogant ignorance.

Returnees can be an invaluable bridge between the cultures of investors and frontier markets. They often understand the best of the entrepreneurial principles and local market realities of both countries. And they may be less hampered by the limiting mindsets that beleaguer their fellow countrymen.

A truly multicultural entrepreneur, who remains curious and humble about what they do not understand of the local culture, will have a far better chance of success identifying or starting profitable businesses in frontier markets.

WORLDVIEWS

Worldviews are collections or bundles of beliefs that tend to exhibit themselves together in specific cultures.

Worldviews are the broadest cultural framework used to understand the underlying beliefs driving business behaviors and responses.

Three worldviews are evident across the globe: 1) Innocence/Guilt, 2) Power/Fear, and 3) Honor/Shame [9]. No society, however, is a pure distillation of any single worldview. If you consider the three worldviews to be the three primary colors (red, yellow, and blue), then every culture and every person is a unique mix of portions of those three colors, a unique shade of purple, green, or orange.

Culture Orientation per Country

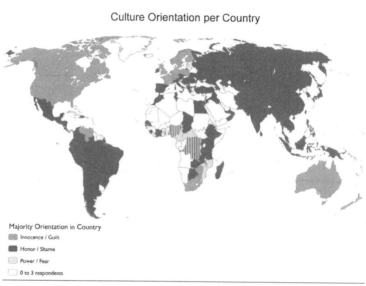

Majority Orientation in Country
- Innocence / Guilt
- Honor / Shame
- Power / Fear
- 0 to 3 respondents

Worldview Culture Orientation (used by permission of Jayson George)

Significant variations often fall along geographic, ethnic, or religious lines, but each country or cultural grouping normally exhibits a dominate worldview. Honor/Shame is the predominant worldview in frontier markets across Asia (including the

---

9. I use the explanations of worldviews and Honor/Shame developed by KnowledgeWorkx and Roland Muller, respectively. "Three Colors of Worldview." KnowledgeWorkx. Accessed December 12, 2017. http://www.knowledgeworkx.com/articles/three-colors-of-worldview and. Müller, Roland. *Honor and Shame: Unlocking the Door*. Philadelphia, PA: Xlibris Corp., 2000.

Middle East) and large parts of Africa and South America. In Europe and North America, Innocence/Guilt predominates. In sub-Saharan Africa, it is Power/Fear.

In addition, there are often shifts over generations. In Afghanistan, for example, individuals who had worked for years with Western companies or organizations would frequently exhibit an interesting combination of their native Honor/Shame Worldview, the Innocence/Guilt Worldview of their workplace and sometimes the Power/Fear of their family's tribal area.

Let's take a look at the three worldviews and their implications for business.

INNOCENCE/GUILT WORLDVIEW

Innocence/Guilt is the worldview that predominates in North America, most of Western Europe, and the Antipodes. It is the water I swim in, along with most investment funds and Western entrepreneurs.

In Innocence/Guilt cultures, the question that drives decisions is most often, **"Is it right or wrong? Legal or illegal?"**

The language used is that of a courtroom. Legal structures, not opinions or public perception, are the measuring stick against which guilt and innocence are measured. Lawyers thrive in an Innocence/Guilt culture.

Every member of society is expected to know the law; ignorance is not bliss. If you are stopped by the police for speeding, any measure of excuses about not knowing the speed limit will not save you from a ticket. Similarly, the rightness or wrongness of an action has very little to do with whether anyone else knows you have done it. You are still guilty even if no one saw you throw trash out of your car window.

Innocence/Guilt cultures rely extensively on contracts. Clear, efficient, and direct communication is applauded. Deductive reasoning is used at every step, and cause and effect are established before decisions are made.

The strong belief in cause and effect brings an expectation that we are in control of events. The locus of control, especially in Americans, lies firmly within the individual. Fate is not predetermined or inevitable.

If you're from the U.S., Canada, Australia, New Zealand, or most of Europe, do you recognize yourself in these descriptions?

President Bush was speaking from an Innocence/Guilt Worldview, when he proclaimed after 9/11, "You're either with us or against us!" and "This is a fight of good versus evil." Our classic movies often have a "good guy" and a "bad guy" and the storyline is about the battle between the two.

The abuse or misuse of the Innocence/Guilt Worldview is "Innocence at all costs." *I must be able to prove my innocence. I must be able to defend my position with facts and logic and a myriad legal precedents.* CYA (cover your ass) finds its way into many decisions and practices.

This is one of the reasons why a significant percent of some Western-run development project costs are consumed by "monitoring and evaluation." In practice, CYA too often becomes more important than bringing truly effective solutions.

HONOR/SHAME WORLDVIEW

Honor/Shame is the predominant worldview in most frontier markets—across Asia, the Middle East, much of Africa, and South America. Understanding Honor/Shame is so important to your success in frontier markets, that we'll explore this worldview in depth in Chapter 4: Honor/Shame Worldview.

The question that drives decisions in Honor/Shame cultures is most often, **"Will it bring honor or shame to my family and to myself?"** Avoiding shame, more so than gaining honor, is woven through every transaction.

Honor is determined by the complex network of relationships in which an individual participates, not by an impersonal law or regulation. Honor is "a good reputation: good quality or character *as judged by other people* [italics added]".[10] The community holds the definition of honor and therefore you are, and must be, continually connected to the pulse and opinions of the community, be it family, clan, or tribe.

Honor/Shame does show up in Innocence/Guilt cultures. Look for instance at the power of being considered "cool" or "uncool" among youth in Western countries. Cool is a form of honor as dictated by the crowd. Cool is not a law or regulation, but an acceptable behavior as defined by the group.

One of the abuses or misuses of the Honor/Shame worldview is "Honor at all costs." (Or sometimes more appropriately, "Avoidance of shame at all costs"). *I must preserve my and my community's honor.* In Honor/Shame cultures, ignorance can be bliss. *How can I be responsible for a law I'm not aware of?* Likewise, because honor is defined by the community, if an action remains hidden or unknown, it will at times not be considered "wrong" by the individual.

POWER/FEAR WORLDVIEW

Power/Fear is the worldview that is strong in much of Sub-Saharan Africa, often mixed with Honor/Shame.

---

10. "Honor." Honor - Definition for English-Language Learners from Merriam-Webster's Learner's Dictionary. Accessed December 12, 2017. http://www.learnersdictionary.com/definition/honor.

In Power/Fear cultures, the question that drives decisions is most often, **"How will it advance or threaten my position of power as compared to others and/or to supernatural entities?"**

In Power/Fear cultures, knowing where you stand in the power structure is paramount. Maintaining your position of power is essential and the use of fear to do so is almost inevitable. A person in a Power/Fear culture will constantly evaluate his or her position in the hierarchy of power within a group or situation and act accordingly. This ability to peg one's position on the power ladder is taught from childhood, as is the drive to move upward.

Hierarchy permeates life, and levels of authority are both known and respected implicitly. Aligning yourself with the right people means you gain power for yourself and for those you lead or are responsible for. In Nigeria, for instance, people will talk openly about the need for a "godfather"—someone with money or influence, who will represent their interests, usually for a price.

Power/Fear cultures are strongly attuned to external powers, often including metaphysical ones. Spirits, fate, and deities play a big part in everyday life and decisions. Superstitious rituals are common and used to appease the spiritual powers in order to maintain the power status quo. Often personal responsibility and initiative are subordinated to those above you, both in the spiritual and temporal realm.

While fear is not inherently "bad" (a certain amount of fear is essential for even good governments to deploy), the abuse or misuse of Power/Fear cultures is "power at all costs." Whatever it takes to maintain power is acceptable. What is "right" is to keep your place in the power structure secure and in doing so take care of those under you.

Power/Fear also shows up in predominately Innocence/ Guilt cultures, just as Honor/Shame does. The military is perhaps the starkest example, though some corporations exhibit it as well. The strict hierarchy and obedience to that structure are foundational components of a Power/Fear culture.

SUMMARY OF THREE WORLDVIEWS

Innocence/Guilt *Elements of Innocence*	Honor/Shame *Elements of Honor*	Power/Fear *Elements of Power*
• There is clear and distinct right and wrong as determined by the law. • There are "good guys" and "bad guys" (classic Hollywood movies). • If innocent, one feels good.	• Honor is in adhering to family or societal expectations. • Focus is on acting "honorably," not necessarily "correctly." • What preserves the relationship is morally "right."	• A person's position within the clan's hierarchy controls his or her life. • There is a never-ending focus on preserving one's place within the hierarchy. • Someone might potentially be able to move up, but it could take years.

Elements of Guilt	*Elements of Shame*	*Elements of Fear*
• An action is judged to be good or bad, even if no one knows it has been done. • It is based on law (from ancient Greek and Roman times). • Wrong depends on standards, not opinions. • Misuse of guilt: 1) "I must maintain "innocence" (i.e., not guilty) at all costs," 2) Creating my own definition of right and wrong (e.g., situational ethics).	• Family/group honor is the guideline for actions. • Shame is to be avoided at all cost. • Performance is more directly linked to worth of a person rather than simply what they've done. • Misuse of shame: 1) "I must avoid shame at all costs", 2) "It is not bad unless I get caught."	• Losing one's place within the hierarchy is only a mistake away. • Aligning with and staying close to the right people is essential. • Misuse of fear: 1) "I have to do whatever it takes to maintain my position/power." 2) Creating fear rather than trust in subordinates.

CULTURAL DIMENSIONS

Cultural dimensions are the building blocks that make up worldviews. They describe more detailed cultural dynamics that span a spectrum, with polarities on each end of the spectrum.[11]

How a culture views destiny is an example of the polarities of cultural dimensions. Do individuals believe life's events are outside their control and dependent on some unseen force or do they feel that they have personal control over what happens to them? These two polarities—or ends—of the Destiny spectrum are seen below.

Destiny[12]

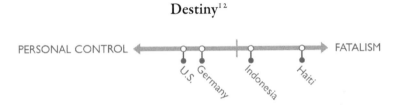

The U.S. and German-speaking countries generally fall near the left end of the spectrum while Haiti, Indonesia, and some other Muslim-majority countries fall on the right side. In the U.S. and Germany, people generally feel that they control more of their destiny than not. In contrast, those in Indonesia and Haiti feel that outside forces, both spiritual and temporal, dictate significantly what happens in their lives.

---

11. For more information on cultural dimensions, including those not explored in this book, check out Marco Blankenburgh's article. "12 Dimensions of Culture." KnowledgeWorkx. Accessed December 12, 2017. http://www.knowledgeworkx.com/articles/12-dimensions-of-culture.
12. Approximate based on a World Values Survey. WVS Database. Accessed December 12, 2017. http://www.worldvaluessurvey.org/WVSOnline.jsp.

The five cultural dimensions below, part of a group of twelve or more depending on the source, are in my view the most important to investing and starting businesses in frontier markets. We will explore these five in the following chapters:

1. Relationship: Community vs. Individual
   ◦ The degree to which individuals within a society value individual accomplishments vs. community coherence
2. Power Distance: High vs. Low
   ◦ "The extent to which the less powerful members of institutions and organizations within a country expect and accept that power is distributed unequally"[13]
3. Communication: Direct vs. Indirect
   ◦ The style of communication when conveying information, opinions, or news
4. Productivity: Task vs. People
   ◦ The value put on relationship orientation or task orientation in producing results
5. Destiny: Fatalism vs. Personal Control
   ◦ The amount of control a person feels they have over events and circumstance in his or her life

Societies or worldviews can be described by where people fall along the spectrum with regards to multiple cultural dimensions. Cultural dimensions allow us to delve further into the detail of these differences. They also allow us to appreciate the variations and nuances that exists within any society.

These dimensions "bundle" together to create a worldview. The illustration below shows where, approximately, the Innocence/Guilt Worldview crosses five representative dimensions.

---

13. Geert Hofstede, *Culture's Consequences: Comparing Values, Behaviors, Institutions, and Organizations Across Nations (2nd ed.)* (Thousand Oaks, CA: SAGE Publications, 2001), 98.

MINDSETS

Mindsets are beliefs that emerge as a result of particular experiences, rather than simply from the surrounding culture itself.

Worldviews and cultural dimensions describe beliefs that are deeply engrained in the fabric of societies, having been passed on from generation to generation. Mindsets, in contrast, are more recently learned beliefs that arise from intense experiences.

The origins of mindsets in experience make them no less powerful. In America, for instance, the pioneer mindset manifested itself on the Oregon Trail as settlers headed west. This mindset still shows itself in the belief that any man or woman can succeed, no matter their origins. Similarly, the experience of chronic poverty, the threat of violence, or the oppression of a tyrannical political system have profound impacts on the beliefs and behaviors of those in frontier markets.

We will explore three mindsets, central to frontier markets, in detail:

1. **Survival Mindset**

   The narrow and all-consuming belief that making it through today and only today is the paramount goal and that all activities, pursuits, and values not directly contributing to that goal are wasted and worthless.

2. **Zero-Sum Mindset**
   The belief that the "pie" of resources (natural and human), power, and even time is static and limited, and that when one person gains in these areas, all others lose.

3. **Limited Possibilities Mindset**
   The belief that the possibilities you see in front of you are the only ones available.

RELIGION

I would be remiss if I didn't include some comments on the topic of religion. While religion is decreasing in its influence and prominence in the West, in most other countries it is a powerful component of the culture. However, the behaviors that come out of any individual religion depend on the worldview mix of the culture where it is practiced. As an example, Christianity's origins were in a predominately Honor/Shame Jewish culture, with a strong Power/Fear overlay from the Romans. Yet Western Christianity has taken on a far more Innocence/Guilt orientation.

Islam takes on the color of the predominant worldview where it is practiced as well. For example, Afghan Pashtuns apply the Quran to their lives through the lens of Honor/Shame, with an overlay of the Pashtunwali cultural code.

Become familiar with the religion(s) present in a frontier market and consider it through the lens of the prevalent worldviews in order to interpret the meaning behind the behaviors you see.

PART II
WORLDVIEWS

MAKING IT ALL PRACTICAL

Let's now dive into the details of how these worldviews, cultural dimensions, and mindsets show up in business. Here is where we look at the practical aspects of recognizing and responding to these beliefs as we encounter them in frontier markets.

These beliefs come out of culture or experiences. The cultural beliefs (cultural dimensions) are the building blocks of a person's worldview. Overlaying all of these cultural beliefs are mindsets, which come out of experiences, especially traumatic ones.

In the next chapters, I have chosen to expand on the one worldview, five cultural dimensions, and three mindsets that are most germane to investing in and growing businesses in frontier markets.

We'll break down each worldview, cultural dimension, and mindset into their component beliefs. Then, we'll delineate behaviors that result from these beliefs. Finally, we'll explore recommended and effective responses for each of the resultant behaviors.

BELIEFS BEHAVIORS RESPONSES
AT THE BY
WORKPLACE MANAGEMENT

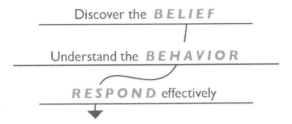

Discover the *BELIEF*

Understand the *BEHAVIOR*

RESPOND effectively

We will start with digging deeper into Honor/Shame, the worldview shared by more than 70 percent of the world's cultures. It is, in many ways, the one that is most different from the Innocence/Guilt Worldview the majority of the readers of this book hold.

Continue to keep the Belief Tool at the front of your mind as you read and contemplate the Honor/Shame beliefs, behaviors, and responses.

CHAPTER 4

HONOR/SHAME WORLDVIEW

A man without honor is like a balloon without air.
All the ingredients are there, but it serves no purpose.

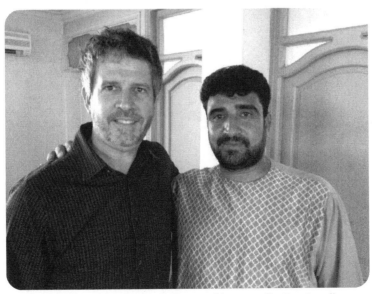

Naseem in my apartment in Herat, Afghanistan (by Curt Laird)

Naseem had been a soldier with the Mujahedeen during Afghanistan's bloody civil war and fought with the U.S. Special Forces against the Taliban. In 2004, he became my driver in the Western province of Herat, where I was busy setting up a cell phone business. Though drivers were not commonly treated as equals in the culture, I made a deliberate decision to treat him with respect. And so it was that on one long night, when the streets teemed with angry rioters, Naseem became my bodyguard.

The Afghan government had just used a security incident to "promote" the local and exceedingly powerful warlord, Ismail Khan, out of his position as governor. A small group of protestors marched on the United Nations (UN) compound and, swelled with ranks of hooligans and thieves, set about burning, looting, and shooting offices and storefronts only a couple of hundred meters from my office and guesthouse. More than at the Afghan government, they were angry at the Americans who they blamed for the move against their patron.

The phone rang and a desperate sounding woman from the U.S. Consulate frantically told me to evacuate immediately. "The mob is hunting foreigners!" she said. I felt the fear start in my toes and rise right up through my body, threatening to swamp my mind. As head of one of the largest businesses in town, I knew I was among the most well-known foreigners in the city. I looked around my room and figured that all was lost. It would all be ash in a matter of hours. Still, I could not go. I had thirty Afghans and three foreigners depending on my decisions and none of them was allowed the protection of the U.S. Army base like I was.

Suddenly, a knock came at my door. There stood Naseem looking like something out of *Rambo*. He held his AK-47 assault rifle and grenades, and extra magazines of ammunition were strapped to his big barrel chest. "I will protect you," he told me, through the translator standing beside him "I will guard the staircase and no one will get by me." If I had not been so juiced on adrenaline, I would have cried.

Naseem had braved the violence-wracked streets to race his car home, pick up his gun and ammo, hide them from any check at roadblocks and make his way back to my front door. As he stood guard through the night in the stairwell to my room, there was not a doubt in my mind that he would lay down his life to protect me and my colleagues. Because of the respect I had shown him, his honor demanded that he protect me with his life.

It is difficult to overstate how powerfully, even fiercely, the drive to preserve honor and avoid shame influences the decisions and lives of people living within Honor/Shame societies. One's honor and that of their family sits at the very apex of their identity and significantly determines their sense of worth. At its most extreme, threats to one's honor are perceived as existential threats for which one should be prepared to fight, sacrifice, and even die. One well-known saying in such cultures: "A life without honor is a life not worth living."

Preserving honor and avoiding
shame influences every decision.

As an investor, entrepreneur, or manager, you have the power to inflate the honor balloon or to pop it in an instant. Both honor and shame are powerful tools, when wielded wisely. How you use them can mean the difference between a successful business and an embarrassing failure.

Honor is a bank account and respect is the currency. Set up an honor bank account for every Naseem in your life. Generously deposit respect in it, and it will pay you back richly. In time, you will be able to withdraw extraordinary amounts of loyalty and hard work. There is no single better place to invest your time and effort.

Shame is a sword that cuts both ways. Avoiding shame, both personal and communal, is the number one priority for those living in Honor/Shame societies. In private, shame can be used to keep people honest. As trust and respect are built, you can appeal to that relationship to call people to account for their failures. Without ever saying the word, the shame of trust betrayed can itself demand a higher level of loyalty.

Shame must be used wisely and sparingly, however. Most importantly, be careful not to publicly shame someone in an Honor/Shame culture. Neuroscientists have found that "humiliation [i.e., shame], which is associated with feeling lowered in status in the eyes of others, is one of the most intense emotions that someone can experience, even when compared with feelings of anger or happiness."[14]

If you shame someone in public, you can be assured of a sharp retribution or punishment. In many cases, you'll never know it, because their retaliation will take the form of sowing distrust, suspicion, anger, or of covertly sabotaging work projects.

Let's look at how Honor/Shame plays out in specific behaviors in different business situations and how you—as an investor or manager—might respond.

---

14. Birrane, Alison. "Yes, you should tell everyone about your failures." BBC Capital. March 13, 2017. Accessed December 12, 2017.
http://www.bbc.com/capital/story/201703 12-yes-you-should-tell-everyone-about-your-failures.

BELIEF 1: WEAKNESS AND FAILURE MUST BE AVOIDED AT ALL COSTS.

"Weakness and failure are shameful and must be avoided."

In the West, failure is increasingly regarded as "the first step to success." Business schools dedicate whole modules to the *Lean Startup* model of "build, measure, learn," central to which is the expectation that a certain degree of managed failure is critical to the success of any business. Our Western bankruptcy laws mitigate failure; acknowledging failure brings rebirth and new chances. Even in my family, we often repeat to our kids the phrase, "Fail fast! Fail forward!" to encourage them to get up quickly after they fail and keep moving forward.

Failure is fatal in
Honor/Shame cultures.

In Honor/Shame cultures there is no positive spin on weakness and failure. Failure is fatal. It is the ultimate show of weakness, and thus avoided most fervently. For those growing up in Honor/Shame societies, admitting failure is seen as a public admission of deficiency. It brings shame on oneself and one's family.

Not only does it bring shame, but, historically, perceived weakness on the part of a tribe or community often brought on attack and subjugation. Weakness could be fatal for small tribes or communities, competing for land or resources. They had to be strong—or at least seen as strong, because the survival of the community was at stake. The weak were (and still are) often shunned. The vestiges of this remain even generations past the tribal days.

The implications of this belief are far-reaching in the investment-management-exit cycle in frontier markets. Accurate information, both good and bad, is at the core of decision making in the initial investment stage and as the business grows. If weakness is shameful, the behaviors below are just a few of the challenges to be met.

WOMEN AND THE DISABLED IN HONOR/SHAME CULTURES

In many Honor/Shame cultures, women and the disabled face a particularly challenging association with shame-as-weakness. While wives and mothers are loved, they are often seen as inherently weaker than men. And while there are a few cultures where the disabled are seen as having a "touch from God", in most cultures they are pushed to the sidelines and believed to be defective and weak.

Overcoming these perceptions is a challenge. We explore this more on page 80.

BUSINESS BEHAVIORS

Behavior: "Bad news" is buried and mistakes are not owned.

"Bad news" is critical to a company's growth and success, because it informs how the company pivots and responds to market forces. For businesspeople and employees in Honor/ Shame societies, however, bad news equates to failure and is deeply shameful. It is extremely difficult for individuals within

Honor/Shame contexts to report failures accurately or to openly take responsibility for their own.

Bad news reflects badly on the bearer, but it may also be seen by the bearer as bringing shame on the person to whom they are reporting. Thus, it is avoided or given in such an indirect way that a person from a Direct Communication culture may never understand the news (we'll talk more about Indirect vs. Direct communication in chapter 7).

The result is that bad news and failure are hidden, often until the worst possible moment. You may be blindsided by the discovery of a very significant failure, if you have not put in place the institutional culture and systems to bring them out into the open.

This tendency to avoid admitting failure or to share bad news is perhaps most lethal when applied to the due diligence stage of an investment or to the monitoring and reporting of corporate achievements and failures. What you see and what you are told may not be reality.

Burying bad news is, of course, not uncommon in the U.S. The difference is that it is usually either clearly and knowingly fraudulent (i.e., illegal and dishonest) or it uses "creative accounting" that technically maintains "innocence," but results in similar damage. It adheres to the "letter of the law" and therefore assuages the right/wrong conscience of an Innocence/Guilt culture. In Honor/Shame cultures burying bad news is far more motivated by maintaining honor than by maintaining innocence.

Even when the stakes are low (in Westerner's eyes), those from Honor/Shame societies can be loath to admit a mistake or to take responsibility for failure.

The generator at our house ran out of fuel one night and so, of course, the lights went out. I waited patiently to hear the pitter patter of *chawkidor* (night guard) feet running to get it going again. But after five minutes there was not a sound. I rose from my seat and made my way carefully through the dark to the chowkidar's annexed quarters in the front yard. Knocking on the door, I heard the unmistakable sound of my chowkidar wrestling himself awake from a sound sleep. When finally the door opened, I said laughingly, "You were asleep, weren't you?"

"No, no, I was studying," he said.

Incredulous, I asked, "The lights went out, the loud generator went silent...and still you didn't notice?"

"No, no, I was closing my eyes to memorize my lessons." Running briefly back into the room, he returned with the paper he was supposedly "memorizing."

He remained insistent no matter how hard I tried to assure him that he would not be penalized for telling me the truth or questioned him on how it was that he had not noticed the lights going out. "No, no, Mr. Curt, I wasn't asleep."

Behavior: You'll rarely hear "no."

The word "no" is not in the working vocabulary of most colleagues and clients in Honor/Shame societies when answering to someone higher up the hierarchy. They may emphatically mean "no"—"no, I don't know the answer to that", "no, I can't do the task you're assigning me"—but invariably it will be pronounced "yes."

This trait is very connected to the principle of "saving face." Admitting ignorance—a "failure to know"—or inability—a "failure to be able to do"—is deeply embarrassing and thus shameful, particularly if one is forced to do so in public.

This reluctance to say "no" also plays out when operating across a language barrier. In an Honor/Shame culture, people will often nod in agreement when you ask if they understand your English. They may have understood the actual question, "Did you understand what I just said", but *not* what you've been talking about for the past ten minutes—though they won't tell you this.

Behavior: You'll almost never be contradicted or told you're wrong.

In Honor/Shame societies, people will work hard to maintain your honor too. The typical schooling system in many Honor/Shame cultures actively discourages critical questioning or any challenges to those in authority, especially teachers. What's more, the hierarchy of age plays out within most families. It actively quiets the opinions and contributions of those who are younger, even when they are more educated or informed on a subject.

If someone tells you that you're wrong or headed in the wrong direction, this exposes your weakness and that is shameful for you. You may eventually fail, but at least the person who didn't correct you can feel good that he did not reveal your shame.

Behavior: Data, especially financial, is primarily used as a tool to enhance honor and reputation, not to accurately reflect reality.

Systems emerging out of an Innocence/Guilt belief framework encourage accurate reporting of the facts and figures critical for due diligence and for making operational decisions. They make little or no consideration at all to the relationships and honor that is at stake, either for those reporting or for those being reported on. This is not necessarily the case in Honor/Shame societies.

In Kabul, a set of audited financials from the local affiliates of international accounting firms can be bought for $5,000. Whatever picture you want the books to paint, they will paint.

And I assure you, they will paint a glowing picture! Weakness is to be covered by any available means.

I had an international investor assure me they were confident of a potential investment's financial health because they had locally audited financials. I almost burst out laughing. International investors, coming from Innocence/Guilt cultures, assume that the financial statements will reflect reality, warts and all. But data is a tool to enhance honor in Honor/Shame cultures. It may not be considered "wrong." It is just the way it must be done, and everyone—except the outsiders—understands that.

EFFECTIVE RESPONSES

Response: Never take data at face value.

At the business accelerator I founded in Kabul, we were taking steps to help an Afghan investor buy a local pharmaceutical plant. The owner sent us the financials. It looked like pure profit. It was all roses and no thorns; the data probably would be considered fraudulent in most developed countries. Of course, any owner anywhere in the world is going to try to make his or her business look as good as possible, but in developed countries there are standards and systems that generally obviate the worst excesses.

Data is meant to enhance honor,
not necessarily reflect reality.

As the decision maker and foreigner, I most likely would never have gotten the real numbers, but, over many cups of tea, my local team got behind the honor veil. We had to essentially recreate the business' accounting system to get to the real numbers. By doing so, we could negotiate a realistic price. In the end, the seller saw that we weren't fooled and backed out of the deal at the signing ceremony. We were saved a potentially disastrous investment.

Data is meant to enhance honor. Every time you see data, think, "This data is meant to enhance honor, not necessarily reflect reality." If you understand the belief behind the data, you will know how to respond.

INVESTOR TIP

When looking at the financial books of a potential investment, realize that there are often at least three versions. First there are the financial books intended for potential investors, then the books kept for tax purposes, and finally the real books, records for which are often not even kept. Not much matches.

If an owner ever pulls out a little spiral notebook from his or her pocket when you ask them a financial question, you can be almost sure that none of the proffered "books" is grounded in reality.

It is not impossible to get to the real numbers (or something very close). To do so, however, requires far more intensive investigation and almost invariably the help of a trusted team of locals, who can ferret out the real information. Put on your best Sherlock Holmes hat and dig in.

Response: Invest in systems that limit opportunities to obscure bad news.

Be creative and invest in systems to uncover the good, bad, and ugly of a potential investment or of the day-to-day health of your business. Focus on making it next to impossible to obscure the truth. Remember, while it might be "wrong" for you not to report truthfully, it is "wrong" for those in an Honor/Shame culture to report in such a way that brings shame to themselves or their community.

Sometimes letting the bad news come to you through a third party will shield the honor of the bearer. As we have said before, as a foreigner, you will never be able to see fully "behind the veil." Find a trusted deputy of local culture and let them ferret out the real news.

Technology too can be a huge asset. In Afghanistan, the introduction of GPS-equipped cameras to monitoring missions radically changed the quality and accuracy of reporting, particularly on construction projects in remote locations. For years previously, photographic "proof" of completed sites were taken nowhere near the requested locations. The same building was shot from different angles and passed off as multiple completed buildings. GPS tagging put a quick stop to that.

A COSTLY CLASH OF CULTURES

The U.S. and other donors have spent more than $100 billion in Afghanistan over the past fifteen years.[15] There's little doubt that this has contributed greatly to improving health care, education, and basic services. It also cannot be denied, however, that a vast amount of this money has served to enrich the private coffers of politicians and well-connected businessmen. Western aid agencies have, understandably, responded by placing increasing emphasis on meticulously tracking, auditing, and monitoring every cent given to development programs. There is a problem, however, as the hundreds of inaccurate and sometimes completely fabricated reports demonstrate!

Corruption is certainly part of the problem; I will deal with it in a later chapter of this book. What is also at play, however, are fundamental differences in the worldviews from which Western donors and their Afghan counterparts operate. It has contributed to reinforcing a fundamentally symbiotic, but utterly dysfunctional, relationship between them and many of those with whom they work.

Most Western aid organizations (as well as businesses) are intensely Innocence/Guilt. The driving principle of Innocence/Guilt cultures is preserving "innocence at all costs." Over the past decade, we have seen the development of ever-more complex and sophisticated efforts to demonstrate, in minute detail, that the aid agencies have done their due diligence. It is, essentially, a cover-your-ass culture.

The problem, of course, is that expats cannot travel widely around Afghanistan due to security concerns, and the Afghans providing the reports operate under a very different mindset. Do you think they will report bad news, when it will reflect poorly on them and bring shame to their community? Not on your life. Thus, reports are issued that paint projects as having proceeded smoothly. The leaders of a given agency are happy with their generally rosy reports, which show they have done their due diligence and have been successful in their endeavors. Local employees get to keep their honor, so they're happy as well.

The lethal mix of Innocence/Guilt and Honor/Shame means that everyone, theoretically, can close out the reporting season happily. Too often, this means that ineffective, inefficient, or outright corrupt programs and partners continue to be funded. It also means that many of the most vulnerable are left wondering where the billions have really gone.

Response: Make lots of little corrections, fail fast, and fail as a group.

Manage shame. Many "little shames" are bearable, especially if they are private and quickly correctable. Coming in a day late

15. Ward, Marguerite. "$100 billion later, Afghanistan is on the brink." CNBC. February 3, 2016. Accessed December 12, 2017. http://www.cnbc.com/2016/02/03/afghanistan-is-on-the-brink-after-us-invests-100-billion.html.

on a one-month milestone won't be hidden for fear of shame and can be corrected without anyone losing face, but six days late on a six-month project may be hidden because it's just too shameful. There will be damage if you go too long and the correction is too big. The mantra of "fail fast" is both good for business and good for relationships in an Honor/Shame culture.

Where possible, fail as a group, including yourself. Try not to assign individual responsibility for failure, if you can.

Response: Redefine "weakness" as simply "not a strength."

Help colleagues and employees understand their individual strengths and how these fit within the team. This brings honor to each person because each is unique in his or her contribution. Not enough of this takes place in Honor/Shame cultures. Instead, building on and maintaining community strengths are always a priority over individual strengths.

Invest time and resources to uncover the strengths of individuals within a team[16]. Encourage individuals to see how particular strengths fill in for someone else's lack of strength. A team member's "weakness" simply makes room for someone with a strength in that area to step in and find great success.

I often use a football (soccer) analogy. One would never criticize a goalkeeper as a "weak goal scorer." He or she *is* weak at scoring goals, but this does not really matter to the success of the team and therefore is not a shame. In the same way, each member of a team has both strengths that add to a team and "weaknesses" that make relatively little difference. Doing

---

16. Gallup's StrengthsFinder assessment (https://www.gallupstrengthscenter.com) is a very useful tool for understanding and maximising individual's strengths as a part of a team, particularly when guided by a professional.

this begins the shift away from seeing personal weaknesses as shameful.

Some weaknesses need, of course, to be turned into strengths. Reframing the weaknesses as something to be worked on, and not to be ashamed of, is a big step toward success.

At the Business Innovation Hub, we ran a StrengthsFinder training course[17] and included every employee, from executive director to driver. Everyone went through the same assessment and every strength was celebrated publicly. One of the most powerful moments came when our youngest driver, who had a speech impediment, stood up and read his strengths out loud. The other employees chimed in with their observations about his strengths and, when his presentation was over, gave him a standing ovation for his courage to stand and deliver. I am betting that had never happened to him before. That kind of recognition is powerful in any culture and doubly so in Honor/Shame cultures.

Response: Teach your employees that bad news is good news.

Never, never assume that your employees will share bad news with you, unless you've trained it into them. How do you do this?

Your response when you discover bad news (even inadvertently) will determine the degree to which a business or team will report it to you later. Make it a point to celebrate failure. This is 100 percent countercultural for many, but it can work if you are consistent and you create a company culture of learning.

---

17. Michael Dauphinee (www.dauphineegroup.com) is a highly recommended international business consultant and coach I've used over the years. He uses StrengthsFinder as one of his leadership development tools.

I use the build-measure-learn cycle outlined in the highly recommended book, *Lean Startup*[18] to reframe failure into something positive. Build your product or service, measure its success or failure very quickly, and then, if it has failed, connect "negative" failure to the positive idea of learning. From the *learn* phase, move quickly back to *build* so the time and scope for failure is limited. Using this build-measure-learn cycle consistently and frequently spins failure into a key component of success and begins to change the beliefs around failure.

You can also use the logic of stories such as Thomas Edison's 9,999 failures developing the light bulb to illustrate that failure is just feedback about what does not work.

Honor those who are willing to talk about and dissect their failures, starting with relatively tiny failures and working towards an environment where even large failures can be looked at publicly. When you respond to failure creatively, seeking to protect the honor of those involved, eventually they will learn how to own failure and leverage it for good.

Response: Own your weaknesses and admit your mistakes.

You will not get your employees to admit mistakes or apologize if you do not consistently practice this yourself. Lead by example. This is tricky, however.

In Afghanistan, the opinions of my local team members differed wildly on this issue. Some were adamant that it would be "fatal" for a leader to admit his or her mistakes or weaknesses. They said, "They will lose respect for you!"

Others, usually the most successful of them, were just as adamant that leaders of successful businesses must create an at-

---

18. Ries, Eric. The Lean Startup: How Today's Entrepreneurs Use Continuous Innovation to Create Radically Successful Businesses, New York: Crown Business; 2011.

mosphere where mistakes and failures are acknowledged and corrected. They admitted that it was risky, but felt it was worth it.

In my experience, the latter is the better course. If you build an environment of trust, respect, and success, any potential "damage" from admitting your mistakes will be more than compensated for by the team's willingness to begin seeing mistakes and failures as stepping stones to greater success. Take the risk.

When building a team, start framing weakness early. Ask every person you interview, "What are your weaknesses?" This generally shocks them and then elicits either, "I don't have any weaknesses," or a litany of non-weaknesses. Explain that you will not consider hiring them unless they can identify and share their weaknesses. Tell them, "You must know your weaknesses to know how to build a team around you."

If the person still cannot or will not admit their weaknesses, I often turn to one of my managers and say, "Since our friend here is having a difficult time telling us his weaknesses, please tell us one of yours." Then I share one of my own. (Be sure to warn your managers of this tactic and explain its purpose.) The potential employees get the idea that weakness is okay from the very beginning.

It's worth noting that admitting your weaknesses can be a particularly risky strategy for female business leaders and entrepreneurs. As I mentioned earlier, women in some Honor/Shame cultures are seen as inherently weaker in the work world. My wife, Katrina, a veteran of cross-cultural interactions around the world, recommends that foreign women leaders and entrepreneurs should be more cautious about revealing their actual weaknesses until their strengths and authority have been well-established and they have developed an environment around them where weakness has been redefined.

As a woman, you will be tested. Start with visible strength. It is always easier to "soften" your response later as you become established. As you show strength, you will often be categorized as a kind of "third sex" (i.e., female and foreign, but powerful) and the hierarchy will be set. Then is the time to have more open conversations about weaknesses.

THE EYES HAVE IT

There are numerous body language cues that accompany culture, none perhaps more important than eye contact. This is of particular interest (and challenge) to women and the younger generation in Honor/Shame and Power/Fear cultures. The point I want to make here is not a do or don't in any particular culture, but as an example of how a behavior can be interpreted based on each person's belief.

Katrina returned to the UK after a stint of working for an NGO in Afghanistan. She was talking to one of her male friends when he said to her, "Do I have something on my shoulder? You keep looking there." Katrina realized that she was avoiding looking directly in a male's eyes, a practice she had picked up in Afghanistan. You might find yourself critical of Katrina for showing herself to be "subservient" to Afghan males by not looking in their eyes, but that is based on your belief of what not looking someone in the eyes means: subservient, cowed, shifty, not trustworthy, hiding something?

In the rural countryside of Afghanistan where Katrina worked, to look a man in his eyes meant you were essentially coming on to him. In Nigeria, to look an older person in the eyes is to be disrespectful, whether it is a man or a woman. Is that your desired effect? Then again, what do you do as a woman leader who needs to communicate the power of your position?

Far more important than memorizing dos and don'ts is to understand the belief that underlies the interpretation of eye contact. Once you grasp that, you can make a wise choice of how to proceed.

Response: Ask open-ended questions.

In the rush to build a national mobile phone business, I desperately needed information quickly and demanded clear answers to my many questions: "Is the contract for the antenna site ready to sign?", "Has the governor been informed of the launch dates?", etc. Yes or no answers, and on to the next question. One day I asked my Afghan transportation manager, "Are we booked for travel tomorrow? "Yes" was his answer. I assumed he knew what I was talking about, but he had not understood my question and was too ashamed to clarify it. I discovered all of this when I showed up at the airport and no company airplane greeted me. I should have asked him, "What time will the airplane show up for our trip tomorrow?"

Do not ask closed "yes/no" questions. Your counterparts will not admit that they do not understand, nor will they directly contradict you. Instead, ask open-ended questions when trying to determine if someone has understood you or if you are following the correct course.

One of the surefire ways to get to the heart of the understanding is to ask your staff or investees to repeat back to you what they heard you say. Affirm what they heard correctly, and gently guide them to a better understanding of everything else you said.

Thankfully, this will become less necessary as you create a culture where it's not shameful to admit weaknesses, lack of knowledge, or mistakes.

BELIEF 2: HONOR FLOWS FROM THE COMMUNITY

"My community is my source of honor; I must always be connected to my community."

In Honor/Shame cultures, individuals' honor and worth are intrinsically connected to that of their family and community. The family/community is their source of both power and protection. It is their life's blood. Community sets the cues for navigating each step in life. The very thought of being separated from one's community may cause deep feelings of dread, fear, and even panic.

BUSINESS BEHAVIORS

Behavior: Every decision must be "endorsed" by the community.

In Honor/Shame cultures, all significant choices, and many minor decisions, are made by or in reference to the extended family and community. You may think you are interacting with an individual businessman or solitary employee, but this is an illusion. He or she is but one face within a community, whether large or small. That person lives and breathes in the context of community and cannot fathom life as an individual actor.

This plays out in fascinating ways. An individual's education and career choices must respect and bring honor to their family. This was the case with a young Afghan friend of mine, who was offered a full-ride Fulbright scholarship to obtain his master's degree in the U.S. It was his life's dream and would set him up for success for the rest of his life. But he turned it down, because his mother was nervous about him going to a foreign country and insisted that he stay to take care of her.

The choices of the community are often accepted without much struggle or heartache, even when they require honoring the wishes of sometimes illogical, fearful or ill-informed patriarchs and matriarchs. It is understood that the good of community trumps the good of any particular individual.

Behavior: Preserving relationships overrides any impersonal law, rule or regulation, or even what is best for a business.

Maintaining honorable relationships is seen as *the* priority in Honor/Shame cultures, including above any requirement to uphold laws, regulations, and other abstract concepts.

The best decision for a company will sometimes (not always) be at odds with the best decision for someone's family or community. Businesses and their leaders can find ways to align these interests or manage their abuse, but it requires careful management.

We saw this numerous times at the business accelerator in Kabul. In one case, we identified the "leakage" of petty cash by one of three owners of a client. However, the other two owners simply would not confront the offender and, in fact, tried to deny that it was even a problem. Maintaining the relationship was more important than plugging the hole. In another case, four owners of a high-potential business were all related through blood or marriage (or both). There was complete dysfunction as three owners seemed to be battling with the fourth for control. But, again, they wouldn't put their issues all out on the table and deal with them. It was almost comical to see the pained faces as they tried to figure out a way to be frank without potentially shaming the fourth. In the end the company collapsed. It was a poignant lesson in the relative value they put on maintaining at least the façade of relationship. I admire their loyalty, which has served them well in so many ways, but great loyalty sometimes cuts both ways.

Whatever preserves the
relationship is morally right.

It is this priority placed on relationship, which itself is linked
back to the ultimate source of worth and identity—the community's honor—that is at play when nepotism or corruption
take place within a company. Three people apply for a job at
your company. One of them happens to be a distant relative of
someone in the company with power over hiring. He may get
the job, even if he is openly unqualified for it. He may get it because your current employee is deathly afraid of being shamed
by his community for not taking care of a "close" relative.

Behavior: Brainstorming falls flat.

We in the West love to brainstorm. It is often our main source
of new ideas and creative solutions to problems. We proclaim,
"There are no stupid ideas." Like magic, the brainstorming
group throws out ideas as fast as they can write. They do so
knowing that most of their ideas are not sensible, practical,
or even doable. They do so also knowing there is little risk to
their reputation and ego. There is certainly no shame if some
of their ideas wind up in the trash bin.

In most Honor/Shame cultures, brainstorming can be a
nightmare. Older employees are loath to risk putting forward
an idea that potentially could be seen as "stupid" or "not good
enough." This loathing is frequently shared by their younger
colleagues. After all, why would anyone knowingly and will-
ingly risk their personal reputation, let alone the honor of the
all-important family and community they always represent?

If, as a Western manager, you succeed in getting ideas out on the table, you are likely to face an even bigger challenge encouraging your colleagues to vote on them.

The first and presiding question for someone from an Honor/Shame society is not, "Which idea is most innovative or presents the best chance of solving the problem before us?"

Instead, very often it is, "Will I shame someone if I don't vote for their idea?" This is especially true for employees who are younger than the owner/originator of a particular idea.

EFFECTIVE RESPONSES

Response: "See" the community behind every action and decision.

In every business and personal exchange, try to "see" your counterpart's family or clan standing behind them, peering over their shoulder and judging their decisions. Their mother will often be the first one in line behind them, followed shortly thereafter by their father and eldest brother. The lines of family members go on and on, extending well into the distance.

When you ask a person to make a decision, visualize them turning to consult the community that stands behind them.

Now every time you ask that person to make a decision, visualize them turning around to consult with the crowd of people standing behind them. This is one of the most effective ways to understand the power of the community in the life of each individual.

Response: Drink tea 'til you pee!

If your bladder isn't screaming from all the tea you have consumed sitting around chatting and exchanging pleasantries, you haven't spent enough time building relationships. Drinking tea is relationship.

Relationship, relationship, relationship. There is no more important word in doing business cross-culturally. Yet, there may be nothing more unnatural to the Western businessperson than taking the time to sit and drink innumerable cups of green tea (or coffee or vodka, if you are in Russia—okay, that one will have to be limited!) without the remotest hint of a business agenda.

Become a master at whatever
mechanism or ritual of
relationship building the
culture uses.

I cannot emphasize this principle enough. Whatever mechanism or ritual of relationship building is used in the culture you are entering, become a master at it. Know that it can be hard to master, not because it is so complex, but because it can seem so purposeless. You will come face to face with the deeply rooted drive for efficiency and speed that courses through our Western veins. We rarely take the time to truly slow down and revel in relationship. Now is your time to develop this worthy new value.

A female expat doctor reminded me: "This drinking tea issue can be difficult for a woman, because there is not always access to a decent bathroom, and we can't just urinate in the street or into a filthy urinal. So we women will try to pace ourselves; we drink the tea, but we can make one cup go a looooonnnnggg way!"

The actual act of having tea in someone's house or office is a very important matter, as it lays the foundation for all future business. An Afghan saying, "*aub wa namak*" (water and salt), expresses this idea well. In the old days when you entered a house, you would drink their water and taste their salt. Once you tasted the salt and drank the water of that family—and survived—you knew you were safe and they knew that you trusted them.

When you have taken the time to build relationships, you enter into the community and suddenly many things become clearer and smoother. You are now part of the honor network that both gets things done and brings richness to your cross-cultural experiences.

Response: Build trust through relationships, rather than relying primarily on contracts or legal language.

Eight of us sat cross-legged on the floor of our first Roshan office building in Kabul. I had searched and negotiated long and hard, and it was time for our new telecom company to sign its first lease. Sitting around that small room were five Afghans and three of us foreigners.

After the lease signing, all five Afghans kept moving around the seated circle so they could be near me. They would then touch my shoulder or put their hand on my leg. My two foreign colleagues laughed at me, but I felt honored. They trusted me. There was not a hint of sexuality in the touch; simply an expression of relationship. I had spent the time to build trust and my Afghan counterparts were showing me it had worked.

Recall the story of the Kuwaiti business owner at the beginning of chapter 3. Within the Kuwaiti's context, relationships were the guarantors of trust, far more than contracts. Just as his South African employee's rigid emphasis on the legalities and details of a contract led to his dismissal, so too can such an approach mean financial and personal disaster for any investor or entrepreneur seeking to do business within an Honor/Shame society.

In many Honor/Shame contexts, the emphasis and importance on relationships can be expressed in ways that may or may not feel comfortable to you as a Westerner. Do remember that such expressions are pure gold, as you move forward together stronger than ever.

Response: In brainstorming, use anonymity as much as possible.

Imagine sitting with a brainstorming group in an Honor/ Shame culture. See the family and community standing right behind each team member? Every idea he or she suggests is a reflection both on them and on his or her family and community. If your team decides an idea is "stupid" or "crazy" or "impractical," it automatically dumps a large measure of shame on the idea giver and on the community he or she represents. Why would anyone risk putting forth ideas? The whole reason for brainstorming falls flat.

One way to compensate for this is to brainstorm using anonymous ideas written down on paper, gathered up, and posted on a white board. Even in Honor/Shame cultures, everyone on your team can hide behind anonymity.

Another way is to brainstorm in smaller groups, making sure the participants know each other very well or are similar in background or age and position. That way, they can feel safer suggesting ideas, voting on them, and then presenting the best ideas to the larger group.

In the end, the best way is to create an environment where crazy ideas are celebrated, where the boss is the lead crazy idea producer, and where creativity is rewarded with honor.

BELIEF 3: ACCOUNTABILITY SITS WITH THE COMMUNITY

"Public or perceived honor is more important than internal or personal integrity."

For those operating from an Honor/Shame Worldview, public or perceived honor is more important than internal or personal integrity.

Unlike guilt and innocence, honor and shame "require an audience"[19]. They are by their very nature outward looking. The power of shame is invoked only when the source of that shame is made public—a stain not only on the individual, but importantly on his or her entire community.

This aspect of Honor/Shame societies can jar those whose beliefs are informed by an Innocence/Guilt Worldview. The Innocence/Guilt Worldview is driven by impersonal rules and laws, which are easily internalized. Something is right whether it is seen or not. A premium is placed on internal, personal integrity, defined as the degree to which there is consistency between one's private and public behavior. It is almost as if there is a little police officer inside, constantly keeping you aligned with the rules and regulations, even when you are completely alone and away from any relationship.

People who operate within an Honor/Shame Worldview prioritize integrity too, but it is the integrity and honor of one's family, community or clan that takes precedence over

---

19. Benedict, Ruth. The Chrysanthemum and the Sword: Patterns of Japanese Culture. Houghton Mifflin Harcourt, 1946.

one's internal or personal integrity. The moral compass within Honor/Shame societies is primarily external, rather than internal or personal. That "little police officer inside" in Honor/ Shame societies is asking the simple question, "Will this bring shame to my community?" The perception of others is an all-important, but highly fluid and often ambiguous reference point for colleagues, clients, and employees within these cultures. What one does in private, by definition, is not part of the story of the community; it has little effect on a community's honor—unless it becomes public.

Behavior: Performance and honesty can suffer when not monitored.

The dark side of the outward orientation of Honor/Shame societies is that individuals may *act as if* they believe that, "It's not wrong if it's not public" and similarly, "It's not wrong unless I get caught." Many, even most, individuals from these societies will insist that there is a right and wrong, and that those standards hold true regardless of whether an action is witnessed or not. In practice, however, the individuals' conscience in an Honor/Shame culture is tightly coupled to the community. Decisions are ultimately driven primarily by the question of whether a particular action will bring shame to the community, should it become public. If something is "technically" wrong, but has preserved the family or communities' honor and relationship, then the greater good has won out.

Performance and honesty will suffer when divorced or distanced from community accountability or watchful, independent scrutiny. Honor is the fuel that powers the engine of performance in Honor/Shame societies. No amount of rules, regulations, or private/hidden incentives will get the engines performing at full capacity. Like filling a truck's diesel tank with gasoline, the engine powering performance quickly sputters and fails.

Response: Set systems in place to micro-monitor performance.

Maintaining a consistent, visible presence is critical to ensuring good performance and honesty. We will call it micro-monitoring (we will explore this in more detail on page 137).

My friend was building an airstrip in the middle of the dense Papuan jungle. He had contracted with villagers nearby to hack down the trees and fill in the depressions, all by hand. As he stood there watching the massive crew of people work with fervor, he knew the airstrip would be built in no time at all.

After a short time, he headed back to his small house to work on other pressing matters. When he returned, he saw that there had been no progress and the entire crew were sitting down on the job. Upon seeing him, they jumped up and started working again. He reprimanded them and then satisfied, headed back home, only to have the same thing repeat itself when he returned. If he was watching, they worked; if he left, they stopped. His frustration rose. There was no way he could watch them all the time and get anything else done.

It so happened that my friend had lost an eye in his younger days and had a glass eye. Banking on the fact that his crew had never seen a glass eye, he took out the eye and set it on a pole near the work area. "I'm watching you," he said, and walked away. When he returned an hour later, the crew was still hard at work. He walked back to his house proud of his creativity. Two hours later he decided to check on the progress and returned only to find the crew once again sitting on the ground doing nothing. As he stood there perplexed, he glanced over to the pole with the glass eye perched on top. Only now, there was a tin can over the eye. The crew had outfoxed him!

As you invest in and grow companies, you must continue to micro-monitor every part of the company, primarily through your physical presence, signifying the all-important relationship. Once you have hired and encultured a trusted set of managers who will take on this task for you, they will, in essence, become your physical presence. Eventually, through success and reward, the new corporate culture will mean less need for micro-monitoring. Even then, do not go long without delving deeply into the details of the business. If you do not, the ship *will* wander off course in time.

Beyond your continued presence, create clear, simple, and very visible systems and processes that monitor performance and responsibility. This level of detailed oversight is a significant investment at the beginning, but it will yield dividends down the line.

Response: Incentivize with honor.

If honor is a bank account, make generous deposits in your employees' accounts whenever they perform well, especially when they do it outside your immediate view. Remember that honor is like life itself; give them honor and they will pay you back in many, many positive ways.

Make deposits in each person's
honor bank account.

Give honor publicly and spread it around. It is counterproductive to create any kind of competition around honor, so find even small ways to honor as many of your employees as possible.

Shamim, my office administrator at the Business Innovation Hub in Kabul, was a young woman from an often-marginalized minority tribe. I would happily build a company around her as her intelligence, integrity, and instinct for business were impeccable. How did I both reward and incentivize her in one powerful way? I named her as the master of ceremonies for our official launch, attended by dignitaries and influential people (mostly male). It may not sound like much in many countries, but in Afghanistan it is an uncommon honor for a young female to be in that position.

I also invited our drivers and interns to take part in interviewing candidates for even the highest positions. This enrolled them in the success of the company and gave them the honor they deserved in the organization. It may seem simple and it is. Remember, honor fills the bank account.

Response: Cultivate the community as your ultimate accountability mechanism.

Community can be your ultimate accountability mechanism. Each community member stands to lose something for the actions of a single individual. As a result, each member of the community acts as a vigilant watchman over the behavior of other members to ensure that the honor of the whole is maintained.

Senior and respected members of the community have particular power to bring discipline and to restore or bestow honor. Know who they are. If possible, cultivate relationships of mutual respect with them. They have the power to exert the ultimate punishment for dishonorable behavior—banishment from the community. While this is unlikely to be a threat you want to or should make use of, its very existence can be a significant motivator and check for performance and honesty. They also have the power both to restore honor to someone and to bestow the ultimate prize—a seat of special honor within the community.

THE RESTORATION OF HONOR

To those of us from Innocence/Guilt cultures, the restoration of honor in Honor/Shame societies is a curious process. In some cases, the shamed person is required to perform an act of contrition or apology similar to what we would do in the West. However, most of the time, the shameful act seems to be simply swept away with a few words from those above. We demand punishment, a penalty, or payment, but people in an Honor/Shame society demand restoration of relationship, a sort of recalibration of the relational equilibrium.

One of my Afghan friends comes from a respected family in a rural province. During the Soviet occupation, his cousin's family went to work with the Soviets. This was a hugely shameful move as the Soviets were not only the hated occupiers, but also the godless Communist infidels. They were the enemy in every aspect. When the Soviets left in 1989, the family returned to their home province in utter disgrace. They were immediately abused and taken advantage of, with much of their land taken and their daughters kidnapped. When my friend's father saw this, he made a decision to stand with his cousin. There was nothing his cousin could do to restore his own honor; someone higher up the ladder—and who had an honor "bank account" full of credit—would need to use his position and his honor "credit" to pay the price of restoration.

Think of the community as a sponge and a shamed person as a drop of water. If the drop stays away from the sponge, it will continue to exist as a separate and "shunned" entity. But the moment the drop moves to the surface of the sponge, the sponge by its very inherent quality, its very reason for existence, absorbs the drop and the drop disappears, losing its identity as something separate. In the same way, the shamed person is "absorbed" back into the community, losing his or her separate "shameful" identity, and everything continues almost as if it did not happen.

BELIEF 4: IGNORANCE IS BLISS

"What I don't know, I can't be held accountable for."

What happens if a police officer stops a driver for going over the speed limit? In Honor/Shame cultures, the speeder says to the police officer, "No one told me the speed limit; I'm not responsible." In Innocence/Guilt, the police officer would say, "You should have known; you are responsible for knowing."

Because accountability is largely external, or outside the individual, so too is the responsibility for knowing the rules. If someone else holds the moral compass then I cannot reasonably be expected to be held accountable for not steering myself by its direction. What's more, an individual is not responsible for knowing the rules. Someone should tell him or her what to do and how to do it, the person thinks.

Behavior: "I carefully preserve my blissful ignorance of rules and regulations."

Why would I seek to discover the rules, if I'm not responsible for the rules and regulations I'm not aware of?

Like all these behaviors, this is not true of every individual in an Honor/Shame culture. Many of them do seek to be informed, especially those who have worked in the international arena. The tendency to remain ignorant is fairly strong, however, especially when "knowing" carries responsibilities that could lead to failure.

Response: Do not let ignorance be an excuse right from the start.

In less economically developed Honor/Shame cultures, the education system generally tells you exactly what you need to know, expects you to fully memorize it, and then grades you on your knowledge of exactly that information. Relatively little inquiry, curiosity, or initiative are allowed in school.

In such cultures, individuals often make a choice that makes complete sense to them. They decide that it's far more important to be in good relationship with the rule-holders, and simply follow their lead, rather than know all the rules.

All this, of course, bleeds over into the work space. What is in front of the employees and has been asked of them specifically is the only thing that matters. "I didn't know" is a ready excuse.

Be very specific with company rules, regulations, and expectations, particularly in the beginning and with all new hires. Ask new employees to write these down and study or memorize them. Do not expect great amounts of inquiry and curiosity in the beginning.

Over time, the key is to create permission and space to be curious and to explore beyond what is in front of the employee. This not only helps with understanding, but also with being responsible for the rules behind the rules. In addition, it helps with creative problem-solving and innovative thinking.

Give tasks and exercises to your employees where they are forced to go beyond what is given them and where they are required to become aware of all the resources available to them. I often started this during the interview process. For some senior manager positions, Destageer and I would hand the interviewee a sheet of blank paper with a high-level expat employee's name on it and tell them to go get a signature from that person. They had no idea who that person was or where on the headquarters campus they sat. We had briefed the expat to initially refuse to sign the sheet and see how the interviewee would convince them. We were interested to see how candidates used the resources available to complete the relatively simple task and whether they would be intimidated by a difficult exchange with a high-level expat.

In addition, I would regularly walk into an employee's office and give them a project with a clear objective, but minimal instructions. Then I'd walk out and see how they went about marshalling the resources to accomplish it.

In any of these situations, when anyone moved outside their own knowledge sphere and didn't let ignorance become an excuse, we celebrated and honored them.

BUILDING AND MAINTAINING YOUR OWN HONOR AND THAT OF YOUR COMPANY

As we expanded our operation in Herat, I became concerned that we weren't getting routine permissions and assistance from the mayor's office. Reflecting on why that might be, I realized one factor was my lack of personal connection with the mayor himself. I was an impersonal outsider to the close-knit community in western Afghanistan. I asked to meet with the mayor and he invited me to his house.

Over the course of several hours, we drank lots of tea and built a connection. I shared part of my life story with him and explained my passion for helping build Afghanistan. I also honored him for his service and took a genuine interest in his teenage son. I could tell he was revising his judgement of me as he weighed my behavior in the moment. At the end of our visit, he told me, "Because *you* are a good and honorable man, I will cooperate with your company."

In most frontier markets, you are seen as synonymous with the company you lead. The company is an extension of your personality, character, and honor. What you do or don't do to maintain and enhance your own honor can directly affect your company's success in Honor/Shame cultures.

This story helps illustrate two final Honor/Shame issues I'd like to address before we move on. We look at them from a broad perspective, because the details could fill another book.

1. How do you build and maintain your *own* honor and that of your company in the wider community?
2. What are the principles involved in interacting with leadership peers and government officials?

We talked about honor being a bank account. You have a bank account with each of your employees and you have one with the wider community. That wider account must also be built up and maintained. If not, it will affect the success of your company in a myriad of ways.

Here are four important ways to deposit honor in your own honor account.

1. Take care of those below you (i.e., patronage) and protect and enhance their honor in the community. They will spread the word and build your honor account. Think of Marlon Brando in the *Godfather* movies, without the violence (see Power Distance Belief 3 on page 156).
2. Establish and maintain good relationships with community elders, showing homage and respect to them, especially to the oldest. This takes time and plenty of tea.
3. Do not be shy about letting the public see your own good works and honorable deeds and that of your company. Do not be ostentatious, but make sure the word gets out.
4. Keep your ears to the ground for any attempts to dishonor or discredit you, especially by anyone you had to let go or had to expose for their corruption or shame. Take quick action to counter these attempts by visiting the appropriate elders and influencers. Think of this as someone trying to hack your bank account and steal your money.

These are a few principles for doing business or interacting with those who are your peers, including government officials.

1. Maintain everyone's honor—There is no more important piece of advice than to have your "honor antenna" up at all times. Constantly act in a way that maintains or adds honor to those you are dealing with.
2. Go to the top—The top of any business, organization, or government department makes the decision, always. Go forcefully and confidently to the top, but do not shame anyone getting there.
3. Use power and (healthy) fear—Do not be afraid to use a dose of power and even fear when dealing with your leadership peers and with government officials, but do not

use it at the expense of honor.

In the early days of Roshan, I would walk into a governor's office with an official, stamped letter from someone up the ranks telling the governor to cooperate with me. In my Innocence/Guilt Worldview, this official document would get me my rightful assistance, but it often did not. Documents are usually not worth the paper they are printed on. I learned, instead, to walk in with all respect due his or her position, but communicate in many different indirect and direct ways that I and my company had a *relationship* with the highest positions in government (or the requisite power). Implicit in my message was the healthy fear that they would pay a price if they got in the way illegally. Use power and fear to back up your position and rightful honor. If you act with power and honor, they will by default treat you as powerful and respected and either help you or get out of your way.

4. Drink tea—You will tire of me telling you to drink tea by the end of this book, but I hope it's a lesson you remember long after you set this book down. Relationships, relationships, relationships!

5. Leverage your local deputy—The best decision I made at Roshan was to hire Destageer as my deputy. Hire a great deputy and leverage him or her. If you have hired right, your deputy will be someone who has a position in the community high enough to have personal experience wielding power and influence with honor. Honor your deputy in meetings and interactions as a peer and trusted colleague. Be sure this person is not seen as an assistant. Remember the veil! Your deputy can see behind it and be an invaluable guide (read more about my invaluable deputy, Destageer, on page 243).

6. Use your foreigner status—Generally, though definitely
   not always, you get some default respect and deference
   simply because you are a foreigner. People will give you the
   benefit of the doubt, if they see you are trying to be
   culturally sensitive and they sense that you truly care about
   their culture. Use this to your advantage, but be aware that
   it is brittle and can come tumbling down quickly if not
   nurtured.

PART III
CULTURAL DIMENSIONS

DIGGING DEEPER INTO CULTURAL DIMENSIONS

As we've seen, worldviews are the broadest cultural framework we can use to understand the culture in which we are working. Each worldview is a "bundle" of beliefs and, as the Belief Tool explains, visible behaviors and actions flow out of these beliefs.

Think of the three worldviews—Honor/Shame, Power/Fear, and Innocence/Guilt—as the three primary colors of culture. Every culture is a unique mixture of the three colors; every person is a unique shade of their cultural worldviews.

Cultural dimensions are the component beliefs that make up worldviews. Though each worldview is made up of the same "ingredients," they differ in the amounts or intensities of each. Understanding cultural dimensions, then, allows us to recognize and articulate specific cultural details. These descriptions allow you to more objectively look at a culture, or a situation within a culture, and understand more fully the dynamics present. With this framework, you can more easily navigate managing time, people, and resources in building a successful business.

Each cultural dimension is a polarity—the two ends of a spectrum of belief. Think of the polarities as "versus"—this vs. that. For example, consider the concept of *destiny* as a cultural dimension, with Fatalism on one end and Personal Control on the other. Different cultures can be plotted from one end of this spectrum all the way to the other end. In general, Honor/Shame cultures are on the Fatalism side of the spectrum, and Innocence/Guilt cultures on the Personal Control side. As we will see in chapter 9, the beliefs underpinning fatalism have a profound effect on how people perform in business, especially in a crisis, and demand a clear response.

In the next chapters, I go deeper into the five cultural dimensions I believe are essential for understanding investment and building businesses in frontier markets. Keep in mind the Honor/Shame Worldview we described in the previous section and notice how each of the five cultural dimensions can be used to describe and understand it in more detail. Notice also where you land on each of the spectrums, and the specific mix of ingredients and intensities that make up your own worldview—and how it may differ from the cultures in which you're operating.

The five cultural dimensions we will explore are:

1. **Relationships: Community vs. Individual**
   The degree to which individuals within a society value individual accomplishments vs. community coherence

2. **Power Distance: High vs. Low**
   "The extent to which the less powerful members of institutions and organizations within a country expect and accept that power is distributed unequally"[20]

3. **Communication: Direct vs. Indirect**
   The style of communication when conveying information, opinions, or news

4. **Productivity: Task vs. People**
   The value put on relationship orientation or task orientation in producing results

5. **Destiny: Fatalism vs. Personal Control**
   The amount of control an individual has over events and circumstances in his or her life

---

20. Hofstede, *Culture's Consequences*, 98.

CHAPTER 5

RELATIONSHIPS: COMMUNITY VS. INDIVIDUAL

Ali[21], my fleet supervisor at Roshan, was loyal, conscientious, and sharp. He was also part of the Hazara ethnic group, which historically has been at the bottom of the socioeconomic ladder in Afghanistan.

I gave Ali the responsibility of choosing drivers for our ever-expanding fleet of Toyota passenger vans, making it clear that there needed to be a mix of ethnic groups and no favoritism shown to any individual family.

A few days later Ali came to me obviously stressed. "Mr. Curt, I can't even walk downtown anymore."

"Why is that?" I asked.

---

21. Name changed

"Everyone, including my father, is accusing me of not looking after my own people when I hire a driver from another ethnic group."

Poor Ali was under tremendous pressure. He had to choose between failure in my eyes and shame in the eyes of his family. There was really no question that his loyalty to his family would trump his loyalty to me, unless I intervened to provide him cover by making it widely known that I— not Ali— was the one choosing the drivers. If Ali could blame it on me, he was absolved of responsibility and, therefore, absolved of the shame of not taking care of his own.

This may look very much like an Honor/Shame story—and it is. As I have said before, cultural dimensions are components of worldviews. In this case, the Community end of the Relationships continuum (see graph below) is very much part of the Honor/Shame Worldview. It also shows up in many similar ways in the Power/Fear Worldview. Innocence/Guilt cultures tend to fall toward the Individual end of the spectrum, though this varies even within each country.

Relationships[22]

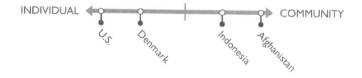

22. Informed by "Compare countries." Hofstede Insights. Accessed December 12, 2017. https://geert-hofstede.com/countries.html and personal experience.

UNPACKING RELATIONSHIPS: COMMUNITY VS. INDIVIDUAL

Most entrepreneurs and investors in the West are less familiar with the Community end of the Relationships spectrum, in my experience. In the U.S. especially, where individualism is celebrated, most businesspeople reside far closer to the Individual end of this cultural dimension.

There is no right and wrong in the beliefs that constitute the Community end of the spectrum, though they may be quite different from your beliefs. The optimum question remains: "Is the belief and behavior working?" As you navigate this cultural dimension, you will find great resource for the success of your investment and business; you will also find challenges.

Let's start with two Community beliefs that are tightly woven together.

BELIEF 1: MY EXISTENCE AND VALUE IS INEXTRICABLY LINKED TO THAT OF MY FAMILY (OR CLAN, TRIBE, ETC.)

and

BELIEF 2: RESPECT AND DEFERENCE MUST BE GIVEN TO THOSE ABOVE ME IN THE GROUP'S HIERARCHY.

As we saw in the Honor/Shame section, in a Community culture—such as Indonesia, Afghanistan and Kenya—the individual barely exists outside the context of his or her family.

This can be a difficult concept to fully grasp for a Western, Individual-culture mind. We in the West were taught from childhood that, for the most part, we are the captains of our own ship, the determiners of our own success. A common life goal is to "become all that I can be." Look at our vocabulary: self-determination, self-actualization, even selfishness.

Replace "self" with "group"— group-determination, group-actualization, group-ishness— and you begin to get a glimpse of how many non-Westerners see the world. Self *is* family. Self *is* group.

People living in strong Community cultures are rarely alone, from the day they are born until the moment they take their final breath. When they sleep, they sleep in a room with most, if not all, of their family. When they eat, they eat not only with their immediate family, but also with their grandparents, uncles, aunts, cousins, and other relatives. Where we in the West treasure our alone time and our personal space, they cannot comprehend why we would choose to be apart from others. They are masters of living in community.

The result of this unapologetically communal lifestyle is that individuals within these contexts understand their value, identity, and very existence as being inextricably linked to that of a larger group to which they belong.

At the far Community end of the Relationships continuum, community works only when people know their place in the structure. Hierarchy is the skeleton that keeps everyone in their proper position. Each individual member knows their place and role within the whole. Should they step out of that role, the structure would become unsound. Thus, hierarchy is preserved and even protected by both the seemingly powerful and the weak within a community.

As part of keeping this hierarchy alive, a system of respect and deference guides you in how to engage with those above you on the ladder. At minimum, your position will rise with age. It therefore benefits you to keep the ladder stable with large amounts of respect and deference. The corollary of this belief is that decisions must have buy-in from those higher in the community hierarchy and from the broader community.

Most of those in Community cultures are baffled by how individualistic the West, and especially the U.S., can be: the pursuit of glory and profit only for themselves and at the expense of others; the excesses of individual competition and ego; children suing their parents; elderly family members put into retirement or nursing homes far away from their children, the people who raised you cast aside in shame. All of these seem selfish and self-serving with no regard for the greater good.

Remember, the Community belief scripts *every* action and *every* conversation.

Behavior: Every significant choice is made in the context of family and community. Decisions made without the buy-in of respected leaders within the family or community will fail.

In Community cultures, all significant choices, and many minor decisions as well, are made by or in reference to the extended family and community, and particularly to respected members therein. This plays out in fascinating ways. An individual's educational and career choices are made not simply on the basis of passion or interest, or even opportunity. Rather, these decisions are made on the basis of what will most benefit the family or community. Individuals must honor the wishes of sometimes illogical, fearful, or ill-informed patriarchs and matriarchs.

This can lead to apparent indecision as the person ponders the wider implications and consequences of the decision on those standing behind them. It can lead business owners or staff to turn down opportunities or assignments that make every bit of sense for their business or career.

You may see something like this happening when you agree with an entrepreneur on a course of action and then find he or she has inexplicably reversed the very next day. Or an employee makes a decision at work, then comes back later to take the opposite position. Mostly likely, he went home to pass the idea by his community only to have it overturned. She may be embarrassed, but there is nothing she can do; the community has spoken and speaks through her the next day.

My friend, Brian Ross, formerly the fund manager for the Afghanistan Business Innovation Fund accelerator, tells a story of the time he was working with a family business in Kabul. A set of brothers ran the company. The younger brother was their translator, as his English was strongest and he could communicate better than his older brother. He would often agree to a specific course of action, then come back later and tell Brian that the decision had been changed, and another course of action would be taken. Over time it became clear that he was agreeing with Brian and his team simply to avoid saying "no" in the moment, but actually was going back to discuss the issue with his older brother, who made the final decisions. Though he was involved in the detail of the family business, every decision had to be passed through his older brother. Needless to say, it was not an efficient process, but it was a cultural reality that had to be dealt with.

Response: Understand that whenever someone speaks, he or she is speaking as "we."

Remember that individuals from Community cultures filter everything through the lens of how it impacts their family, clan, or tribe. The person standing in front of you appears to be an individual, but in actuality, is standing before you as the representative of a community, whether small or large. He or she lives and breathes in the context of community and has no context for life solely as an individual.

See the person standing in front
of you as a "we", not an "I."

Response: Build into decisions the time and process for outside consultation.

Give the entrepreneurs and employees you are working with the time and space to make important decisions, knowing they must take the options back to their community for consideration and approval before they can make a final decision.

In some cases, especially with young or female entrepreneurs, it will seem like every decision must be approved by an older (or male) family member. This is not true of every decision made by employees, but applies to any that may affect them personally.

Don't be harsh when an employee's or entrepreneur's decision is retracted the next day. Instead, acknowledge the cultural reality and build steps into the decision-making process that allow them to get the necessary buy-in. Most of the time this simply means not asking for decisions until they have had "home time" to discuss it with appropriate community or family members.

BELIEF 3: I OWE MY FAMILY MY HIGHEST LOYALTY.

Precisely because one's group identity is so intrinsically wound into one's sense of self, there is almost nothing a person in a Community culture won't do to protect and take care of his or her family and, by extension, their tribe. It is important to understand this when dealing with issues of integrity and honesty. No matter how much respect and honor you have built into your relationships, if you force your employees to make a choice between preserving their family's honor, safety, or survival and being loyal to you and the business, you will lose. They will choose family *every* time.

Never force a choice between
your business and their family's
honor, safety, or survival. You will
lose every time!

In Afghanistan, one of my employees hatched a scheme to defraud the company. His cousin, one of my young managers at the time, knew about it, but could not turn him in to me, at least not directly. When he came to me in an oblique manner, never saying the person's name, I read between the lines. That he even came to me was a sign of real integrity, but he made me promise that his name would never be attached to the accusation. By never having told me the perpetrator's name directly, he could deny ratting out his relative. If it had come out that he disclosed the name, the young manager would have been hounded mercilessly as a traitor to the family, even though everyone knew the cousin had defrauded the company.

Little did I know that I was only scratching the surface of the family politics that this case would involve. I didn't fully understand the power of the family code until my deputy made contact with the son of the provincial governor, who had power and extensive connections, to help us straighten out the situation.

By the time the governor's son was asked to intervene, we realized that two more employees were in on the scheme, both of them distantly related to each other and therefore related to my deputy. The first question the governor's son had for my deputy was, "Which of the two culprits is your closer relative?" He knew that he had to help me in some way by apprehending at least one of them. It didn't matter who the ringleader was; what mattered instead was preserving family honor and allegiance. The second cousin was turned in; the ringleader was fired from the job, but walked free of prosecution. The power of blood trumped all else.

Behavior: Family allegiance inspires both great loyalty and great betrayal.

A common Afghan saying goes, "Me against my brother. Me and my brother against my family. Me, my brother, and my family against my clan. Me, my brother, my family, and my clan against outsiders." Family will win every time if ever there is a clash between preserving individual, corporate, or family honor!

The importance placed on the family or group unit can be a powerful force for both great loyalty and great betrayal. It can be the reason your staff or colleagues will lay down their lives for you once you become "family." In contrast, it can be the reason even your most trusted employees may steal from you, if it comes down to preserving their family's well-being or ensuring its survival. Family allegiance can also prevent theft, if people know their family's honor is at stake if they are caught.

Be particularly aware of the risks when financial difficulties are present for those with whom you intend to work. The pressure will be tremendous for them to provide in any way necessary. Very often, you will not hear directly that there is a problem. If you know the person's family or community, you will learn to read between the lines and will be far more likely to spot the threats.

Response: Invest in relationships with the family, and particularly with the elders, of key employees.

As an investor or manager, your single greatest barometer of risk and your most powerful protection against it is your ability to understand and capitalize on a relationship with the family or community of those with whom you work.

Similarly, as a manager, the greatest way to ensure the continued loyalty, honesty, and hard work of key employees is to ensure that they *and* their families are taken care of. Make a point of visiting them and asking about them. It is, in fact, quite similar to the old *Godfather* days where the head of the business went to the christenings, weddings, and funerals of his employees' families. Loyalty and accountability were built through the web of relationships. It may seem anachronistic to many of us from the West, but these practices are actually expected in Community cultures.

Response: Tie workplace honesty and rule keeping to family loyalty and honor.

The upside to all of this is that if you get the family on your side, especially the elders, you will be far more certain that their sons and daughters will be honest. The latter will think long and hard about not bringing shame on the family.

Remind employees in direct and indirect ways that you have a relationship with their families. Ask about them and mention them in conversations. The connection between their behavior and their family's honor will be made without them consciously thinking of it. That's how strongly the Community belief is woven into the fabric of their lives.

BELIEF 4: SIMILARITIES ARE THE STRENGTH AND GLUE OF A COMMUNITY; DIFFERENCES WEAKEN AND THREATEN THEIR SURVIVAL.

The word "community" has at its root the word "common." This relates to a group having a common heritage, language, religion, etc. In Community cultures, it also alludes to the belief—often unspoken or unacknowledged—that differences weaken the community and therefore should be abolished or avoided at all costs.

Behavior: Individual differences within a group or team are minimized in order to preserve the group identity. Individual personalities and strengths are often not recognized, much less, celebrated.

Innocence/Guilt cultures almost always land on or near the Individual end of the Relationship spectrum. In these cultures, individuals tend to define themselves by how unique or different they are within a group. In Community cultures, however, individuals are more hesitant to highlight their individual differences. Instead they celebrate the similarities they have with their community.

The result of this in Community-dominated teams? Often, there is a muting of individual skills and strengths. You will observe great team loyalty and even well-bonded teams, but organizations often miss out on the important contributions of individuals working in their strengths. They are not efficient and do not operate optimally because there is little appreciation for or value given to the diversity of skills, talents, etc.

Response: Use assessment tools such as Wiley's Everything DiSC® *and Gallup's StrengthsFinder to show how each person is unique* *and valuable within a team.*

Wiley's Everything DiSC®[23], a personality and behavior assessment tool, and Gallup's StrengthsFinder[24], an assessment of individual strengths, were consistently two of the favorite leadership assessments we used at each of the companies I started. They show each team member's unique personality, strengths, and contribution within a team. Without fail, every time I employed these tools, each person that completed these assessments grew in confidence, as they saw how their uniqueness benefited the team.

Encouraging and empowering individuals within a team is a common responsibility of leaders in many countries. In Community cultures, it will be critical that you make it a concerted and continuous effort. Your team members won't naturally know about or celebrate their uniqueness.

You will have to point individual value out publicly. Tie people's uniqueness into the success of the whole team. The football (i.e., soccer) analogy we used previously is useful; each position on the team is critical and each plays a unique role in the success of the team. You will enjoy the best of both worlds if you honor the strengths and contributions of each team member, while concurrently encouraging the cohesiveness of the team as a football coach melds the various skillsets into a team.

---

23. http://www.everythingdisc.com
24. http://strengths.gallup.com/default.aspx

BELIEF 5: COMMUNITY MUST BUY IN TO ANY PROJECTS OR PRODUCTS THAT ENTER THEIR DOMAIN.

My father- and mother-in-law are both public health doctors with years of experience working in Sierra Leone, Papua New Guinea, and numerous other developing countries. They told me about a health training program in South America, where hundreds of traditional community midwives were trained in modern childbirth procedures and then sent back into their communities. To the trainers' surprise, no significant decrease in newborn mortality rates occurred.

An anthropologist followed these community midwives back into the community. She discovered that the older women and religious leaders rejected the new methods because they didn't fit with their deeply held beliefs and generations of experience. The newly trained midwives couldn't put up a fight; they had been overruled by the community hierarchy.

Behavior: Outside ideas, programs or projects are rejected when prior community buy-in is not obtained.

The community acts as a single organism. When anything external wants to enter, it must have the permission and blessing of the heart of the community, not just from one member.

Great products, services, and even businesses themselves have failed because the business did not get buy-in from the community or communities involved or affected.

Response: Spend the time and effort to get community buy-in for projects or programs that affect the community.

Many times, you will need to engage directly with the broader family or community and persuade them of the merits of a particular program or business endeavor. Other times, you will have to work indirectly through members of the community who can sell the idea to the broader group.

The time and effort may seem inefficient—and it is in the short run. You will, however, save yourself incalculable time, money, and headaches if you do whatever is necessary to include the entire community in important decisions that will affect them in even the smallest ways. You most likely will not be told which decisions need community buy-in, but you will learn how to discern them if you stay attentive and curious.

ONE MORE THING: UNPACKING INSIDE-THE-BOX THINKING

Before we move on to the next cultural dimension, let's explore a critical characteristic that rises primarily from the beliefs associated with the Community end of the Relationships spectrum: *Inside-the-box thinking.*

Put an inside-the-box thinker at the wheel of a sailboat on a stormy and icy night and tell him to sail straight ahead. Returning to the wheel several hours later, you will find him with ice in his beard, hands frozen to the wheel, loyal to the end, with a smile on his face—and the boat sailing ninety degrees off course.

Ask him what he has been doing and he will proudly tell you that he has responsibly held onto the wheel and steered straight ahead as promised. What has happened, though, is that the wind has slowly shifted and he has not compensated. He has not adjusted because his rote education does not allow him to think outside of "orders given, orders obeyed ... exactly!" He has no idea how to compensate for unexpected factors as a result.

My experience with inside-the-box thinkers is that you give them a job to do and they will, with joy and fervor, head in the direction you have pointed. Then some small variable will enter the equation and chances are high they will either not see it or have no idea how to correct for it.

Take this story from my friend, Brian Ross. Brian had a beautiful garden space in Kabul, and he wanted to begin composting. He asked his chowkidars to build a small compost bin, and told them about the ingredients that needed to be added to get a healthy compost that would improve the garden's soil. In addition to grass clippings, Brian instructed them to collect the vegetable scraps from the kitchen and throw them into the bin. He tossed in that day's vegetable scrap bucket, which contained potato peels, off cuts of peppers, and some old lettuce, but there were no carrot peelings.

A few days later, after peeling a bunch of carrots, he threw the peelings into the compost pile and mixed it up with a shovel. Later that day, one of Brian's chowkidars came to him and said there was a problem with the compost. Someone had thrown some items in there that did not belong. He proudly stated that Brian shouldn't worry, though, because he'd spent several hours going through the compost pile picking out all the items that did not belong. He then opened a plastic bag that was, of course, full of the carrot peelings that Brian had thrown into the bin earlier that day.

Brian realized that this chowkidar had done exactly what he had been shown. Since there were no carrot peelings in the vegetable scrap bucket on the first day, he believed that the only items that should be thrown in the bin were the ones Brian specifically showed him.

Judge him as stupid and you lose any chance for learning. See him simply as a product of his culture and experience and you gain the opportunity to shift his inside-the-box thinking.

Most people growing up in a strong Community culture have grown up never being allowed or taught how to think outside the box. This does not mean they are bad employees or that you are a bad leader—only that you need to check in on them frequently and train them to take risks and think creatively.

At times inside-the-box thinking comes from a fear of looking stupid or a fear of failure. *Nobody* wants to experience shame. That is true around the globe.

A popular business motto a generation ago in the U.S. was, "Nobody has ever been fired for buying IBM." IBM was the behemoth computer company with a reputation for solid, if not spectacular, products. If you went with an unknown, innovative manufacturer and it failed, you would be blamed. If you went with IBM and it failed, people would blame IBM, not you. Being safe was valued over innovation.

This attitude negatively affected risk-taking in a developed country generally known for rewarding risk. Just think of what it does, then, in a country where failure is shameful.

Below and over the next few pages, I am going to unpack two important beliefs that result in inside-the-box thinking. I will list the two beliefs together and then follow with the common business behaviors and effective responses to those behaviors.

BELIEF 1: I AM EXPECTED TO DO AS I'M TOLD AND WILL BE PUNISHED IF I "COLOR OUTSIDE THE LINES."

For those from cultures that emphasize the community, childhood is filled with reminders that they are to be seen, but not heard. "Listen! Don't talk!" Observe a classroom in Afghanistan, Indonesia, Nigeria, parts of southern and eastern Europe, or almost any nation in the developing world and you will see this at play. The teacher speaks and the students repeat. Students are very seldom permitted to question their teachers, let alone cite additional facts or express original thoughts. Lessons are learned through endless, rote memorization.

These powerful messages from childhood are translated and reinterpreted into behaviors and expectations in adulthood. For the throngs of people outside the circle of authority, literal, unimaginative obedience is expected and attempts to color outside the lines, or to challenge the accepted ways, are punished.

To be fair, respect for elders and those in authority can also be a strength. Those under you will take your orders and direction without much complaint. This is highly valuable in a crisis and during times when you simply need things to get done quickly without a great deal of discussion.

As a result of this belief, people in these countries can barely fathom the disrespect often shown elders and teachers in the West. Outside-the-box thinking is a strength, but every strength is a double-edged sword and your greatest strength can also be your greatest liability.

BELIEF 2: I MUST DEFER TO THE NORMS, TRADITIONS, AND EXPECTATIONS OF MY ELDERS—EVEN IF I HAVE A BETTER IDEA.

This thinking is often controlled by an older generation that, almost by definition in more traditional cultures, will hold older, less innovative ideas and solutions. The "box" in "inside-the-box" is the collective thinking of the community. The locus of accountability is primarily external to the individual and held by the community.

By contrast, within Individual-based cultures the accountability is internalized and therefore not tied down by the traditions and norms of the community. The danger of this is, of course, that individuals are far more likely to head off in directions that are appealing to them as an individual, but not advantageous to the company.

Behavior: People have difficulty responding quickly to unusual circumstances in community-oriented cultures.

Inside-the-box thinkers love checklists and rigid guidelines. If something appears that is not on the checklist, or doesn't fit easily in a known rule, it is not factored into the equation. It can't be. The results of this thinking, however, can be disastrous.

My father is a pilot. He trained Indonesian pilots in jungle flying. These pilots were smart and motivated, the top 1 percent of the professional class. He would give them checklists to memorize and follow; they would pass with perfection, every time.

Then he would throw in a simulated emergency that had no specific checklist. The Indonesian pilots would fall apart in trying to respond to the situation. They were utterly paralyzed, searching for a checklist that applied while the airplane headed rapidly toward disaster.

It wasn't their fault. Their education system prepared them to be master memorizers and *never* rewarded them for thinking outside the box.

This lack of adaptability and nimbleness bodes ill for business. Frontier markets are volatile by nature, especially due to political forces. The ability to pivot is critical, but does not come naturally to an inside-the-box thinker.

Behavior: Creativity is absent.

Inside-the-box societies are subject to the tall poppy syndrome. When anyone sticks their head up, the community cuts them down to size. If you grew up in a place where individual attention was frowned on, you would keep your head down too. Any new ideas or solutions you had would stay right where they were safest—in your head.

It's the tall-poppy syndrome; anyone with new ideas gets cut down to size.

Your colleagues or employees will struggle to be creative. By definition, creativity is about something new. Inside-the-box thinking never creates something new.

Behavior: Brainstorming doesn't work, at first.

Effective brainstorming, by its nature, is looking for solutions that do not appear naturally. A willingness to suggest ideas that seem crazy and illogical often results in finding creative solutions. Brainstorming comes fairly easily to Westerners because they've seen it done and often have participated in it. It is largely unknown and rarely practiced in frontier and emerging markets.

Brainstorming by definition assumes that 90 percent of the ideas are not viable, not practical, or just plain crazy. That is, they are failed ideas. Where inside-the-box thinking exists, failed ideas carry the potential for shame ("If my idea is one of the many 'failed' ideas, it will heap shame on me"). So, brainstorming isn't popular—until you make it so.

You may be wondering why I emphasize brainstorming (and the underpinning of creativity) throughout the book while emphasizing execution less. I find that good, basic execution usually aligns quite well with the cultures and characteristics of frontier markets: dogged determination, persistence, following clear instructions without significant variance, discipline, "just do it" mentality. What needs attention in inside-the-box culture is the ability to come up with the ideas to execute and varying the execution when obstacles arise.

Behavior: Projects slowly drift off course over time (if not watched carefully).

The sailboat story above is a classic example of how projects can slowly drift off course. All goes well when the variables in a project are known and consistent. When some unexpected variable arises, however, it is either not recognized or ignored. It doesn't fit inside the box of what has been memorized.

Behavior: Old solutions continue to reappear.

Copycatting is rampant in frontier markets. This is not "I'll copy the idea and improve on it." It is usually pure copycatting. If you go downtown in most frontier markets to buy bags of cement, you will come upon ten shops, lined up in a row, that look exactly the same—right down to the brand of cement and the proprietor sitting in front having tea. The way it was done is the way it will be done. Old solutions may be refreshed, but new, innovative solutions are rare.

Much of business in frontier markets is simply transactional, not entrepreneurial. Products may have changed over the millennia, but the simple, buy-low-sell-high transactional nature of business has not.

Before we get judgmental about old solutions being tried over and over, let's take a look at the many Western aid and development programs around the world. The same tired programs reappear year after year for decades even though such programs have been shown to be minimally successful, ineffective, or worse. I can't count the number of "women's economic empowerment" programs that train women to make low-quality and monotonous handicrafts that wind up sitting unsold in a shipping container somewhere in the West. As soon as the aid money runs out, the women are out of work because the demand was never there. As the UK's Overseas Development Institute says, "[International development] organizations... tend to be accepting of conventional failure but not of alternative approaches."[25]

---

25. "Adapting design, adapting programming." ODI. Accessed December 12, 2017. https://www.odi.org/events/4146-adapting-design-adapting-programming.

INVESTOR TIP

The fact that old solutions continue to reappear is an opportunity for investors. In many cases "new" solutions for frontier markets are simply tried and true solutions already at work in developed markets. Combine these developed-world solutions with inter-cultural intelligence, and you have the seeds of success.

One clear, yet very simple, example of this is the long-standing practice in developed (and even most emerging) markets of a disciplined sales function in a business. This is rarely true in frontier markets. At the business accelerator I ran in Kabul, not a single client had a sales system in place when we took them on. When we combined a sales system with the valuable relationship components of the Community culture, we saw almost instant sales increases at our client businesses—20 percent in one month in the case of a commercial bakery client we advised.

Response: Find outside-the-box thinkers.

You **must** master the skill of finding outside-the-box thinkers. Find the "gems." This is true if you are looking to invest in a new startup or buying a stake in an existing company and growing it up. You need a core of men and women already well on their way to creative thinking. They will reach new levels of creativity if you use the effective responses below, but you will struggle unless they have a basic foundation. They are also the best "mindset shifters" for those around and below them at the company.

There are no hard and fast rules about where to find a pool of potential candidates, but here are a few tips. Generally, the younger the better. Especially for those working in government, their creativity and innovation will have an inverse relationship to the number of years they have worked in "the beast." Seek out those who have worked for international, especially Western, companies or organizations. Local universities can be a good place to look. Be aware that in many cases, a student's success in these universities depends far more on raw, rote memorization than on creativity. On the other hand, those who have studied in North American or European universities will be far more likely to have developed their creativity and critical thinking "muscles."

There is no substitute for good interviewing practices or for putting in the time to interview en masse. When I went to the western Afghan city of Herat to launch the mobile phone system there, I did more than 220 interviews to hire for twenty-two positions.

I set myself up in the local Herat hotel and interviewed at times for ten hours straight. I was looking for every position needed in a mobile phone system startup: technicians, accountants, customer service reps, logisticians, corporate and inside sales reps, administrators, etc. I created a system whereby in the first five minutes of the interview I rated every candidate from *one* to *five* on meta factors (confidence, basic experience, communications, etc.). Mostly I just looked for good people who communicated that quickly. In those first five minutes each person received a preliminary rating. If they were a definite *four* or *five*, I would end the interview quickly with a promise they would get another interview. Out of respect for the *ones* and *twos*, I would make sure they felt like they had their say and then dismiss them gently. I interviewed the middle-rated group more extensively to see if they would move up to a *four* or down to a *two*. In this way, I got a good overview of the pool of talent available.

The effort was worth every one of the many hours I spent. When I returned to headquarters in Kabul after launching the business in Herat, this group continued to grow the Western region into the largest and highest-quality region in Roshan, and all of it without direct expat supervision.

My point in detailing this simple process is to emphasize the intentionality of the interviewing process, and the hard work it entails for success. Far too many times, the interview process is curtailed in frontier market situations because of its difficulty or the "warm body" mentality. Yet, it is crucial in these markets to identify and recruit the right people.

Use behavioral[26] (asking how the interviewee handled past events) and situational[27] (asking hypothetical or future-oriented questions) interviewing techniques. This is important in the West and *critical* in frontier markets. One of the situational interview questions we used at the Business Innovation Hub was the following: "There is a pot of gold on Paghman Mountain [just outside of Kabul]. Tell us how you would go about getting the gold."

A simple question, but oh so revealing. Not one interviewee ever asked us the most basic question: "How much gold is in the pot?" Some would put their heads down and give up without even attempting to answer it. Those who did answer revealed many different strengths and weaknesses by their proffered solutions. If any gave solutions that addressed even two out of four areas of concern—terrain (including political),

---

26. Behavioral interviewing questions ask how the interviewee handled past events. Here are some sample questions: https://www.thebalance.com/top-behavioral-interview-questions-2059618

27. Situational interviewing questions ask hypothetical or future-oriented questions. Here are some sample questions: https://resources.workable.com/situational-interview-questions

team, timing (i.e., process), and equipment—they were worth a further look. It seems simple, but many didn't even expand on one of those and seemed to simply be waiting for us to tell them what to do.

In each step of the interview process, identify those who exhibit even a seed of creative and courageous thinking. Beyond the search for the usual characteristics of good entrepreneurs or employees—including integrity which is so difficult to assess in an interview—the three most important qualities I look for in a frontier or emerging market employee are:

1. Outside-the-box, creative thinking (or the seed of it, at least)
2. A learning mentality
3. Drive for something different

It is a numbers game in many ways. In frontier markets you will be inundated with applicants. Finding the gems is time consuming, but absolutely essential. Interview, interview, interview! You won't be sorry.

Response: Reward risk-taking and celebrate failure. Create an environment where crazy ideas are acceptable.

There is very little risky about inside-the-box thinking. To encourage outside-the-box thinking and risk-taking, reward employees who take a risk by trying, or even suggesting, a new way to do something. Find out each employee's preferred method of being rewarded. Then, whenever they risk something—even in small ways—give them a reward in their preferred way. In almost every instance, you will also want to include public honor as one of the rewards.

Take the shame out of failure by celebrating failure whenever possible. This, of course, is a valuable and desperately needed practice even in the West. Even more so, it needs to be done in cultures where failure is seen as shameful or even deadly.

Here's a family example that often works effectively in Community cultures. We would never admonish a toddler who falls down repeatedly. Instead, we recognize that they are learning and encourage them to get up and keep going. Think of how long it would take a baby to walk if we yelled at them and shamed them for falling. Why should it be different when learning how to fail well in business?

If someone failed fast or failed forward, reward them. It may shock them that you would actually reward a failure, but the lesson will be deeply felt.

One of the best ways to reward risk taking is to actually try out a seemingly crazy idea. They don't have to be big, crazy ideas at first, but they need to be crazy and outside the box. Try them and then reward the idea giver regardless of whether it works.

In the days immediately after the fall of the Taliban in Afghanistan, there were no billboards, very little radio or TV advertising, and almost no brand awareness. Our team of merry "mobileers" at the Roshan office in the city of Herat decided to get a bit "crazy" in order to get out the good news of a new mobile company. (What may not seem crazy in the U.S. was unheard of in Herat.)

We commissioned two hand-drawn cloth banners of the type that usually hung across the road on special holidays and taped them to the side and back of our employee transportation van. Away the team went down the road to the center of the city, honking their horn and handing out juice and water to the traffic police as they went. Every eye turned to this strange sight. We literally had mobs of people surrounding the car each time we stopped trying to find out what was being offered. Sales went through the roof! Suddenly the team was operating outside the box—and loving it. They came to be known as the most innovative regional group in all of Roshan.

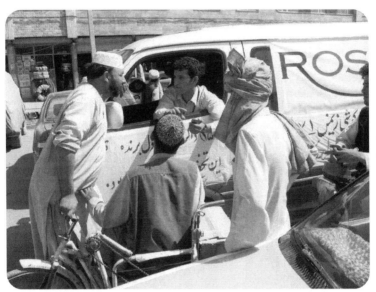

Guerrilla marketing at its best in Herat, Afghanistan (by Curt Laird)

Response: Don't let your team settle for easy or tired solutions.

Getting your team to come up with creative ideas will take extra time. You'll need to be disciplined in sending them back to the beginning until you're sure they've explored all the options. Once you've set the precedent of *not* accepting inside-the-box thinking, it will become easier for them to learn how to hop out of it.

At the Afghanistan Business Innovation Fund (ABIF), Brian Ross said he often used the phrases "Engage our brains" and "Where's the evidence?" whenever he felt like the staff were being intellectually lazy or thinking too inside the box.

"I challenged my staff to think step by step about something they were saying (whether it was the same old ideas of program management or some crazy conspiracy theory)," Brian said. "We regularly held 'Engage our brain' sessions that were a mix of brainstorming; logical, step-by-step thinking and planning; and rational deduction exercises. It soon became a common refrain in the office."

The behavior scaled quickly. "As the staff became comfortable with each other, they began to challenge each other as well," Brian recalled. "It enhanced their ability to critically analyze situations, creatively come up with solutions, and reorient their thinking to fit changing circumstances. I felt its largest impact was in teaching the staff to think beyond how they had been taught in school to think and process information."

Don't stop, don't give up, and don't get impatient. Inside-the-box thinking is often rooted all the way back to childhood and is actively reinforced all the way to the present. It will not go away quickly or easily, but the effort is worth it both for your company or organization and for the country you're in.

Response: Teach your colleagues and employees how to brainstorm.

We've discussed the challenges of brainstorming in Community-oriented cultures, or those operating from an Honor/Shame Worldview. Brainstorming is still one of the best ways to generate new, creative and sometimes 'crazy' ideas. Make it a game. Have fun. Celebrate the craziest ideas. Be the one who throws out the first "failed" idea. Laugh about them.[28] When a brainstorming exercise leads to an unexpected or unusual solution, point it out. Honor the person who got that particular idea going. Then keep honoring him or her in the days that follow.

---

28. There are many good resources for brainstorming online. One I like: https://www.mindtools.com/brainstm.html

It may be helpful, especially in the beginning, to allow your employees to avoid putting their names to new ideas. This lessens the possibility of shame and is worth considering to get the creative juices flowing. I don't recommend this long term though, because you want to develop the confidence to voice even crazy ideas.

Building a culture of creativity is of paramount importance. Organized brainstorming is important, but you will know you have succeeded when brainstorming happens within individual brains in every facet of the business.

Response: Micromanage (or micro-monitor).

Until you're sure that your team has developed the ability to think nimbly outside the box, you will have to micromanage. Every management book in the West tells you *not* to micromanage those under you. Be ready to ignore that rule—at least for a while—in frontier and emerging markets.

I like to use the term "micro-monitoring" to describe the approach that is often necessary. Micro-monitor your employees, entrepreneurs, contractors, and even partners until you are all aligned on behaviors.

This micro-monitoring is going to look different in every situation. It may mean more frequent check-ins, more detailed checklists, or more management-by-walking-around. But whatever the situation, in the beginning, you must be involved continually with the people and projects under you, in a detailed manner, contrary to the normal laws of efficient management. Your colleagues and employees are not being stupid, stubborn, or rebellious, but do need outside input on a regular basis to stay on course until the new territory becomes more familiar.

Ignore the rules: you must
micro-monitor—for a time.

Despite the work of your loyal sailing helmsman, you must stand near him and, as the variable winds come up, train him how to compensate for them. This may seem like wasted time, but he will learn quickly and you will not need to micro-monitor forever.

Inside-the-box thinking will not be true of every person in a given country where it prevails. Find the gems who are outside-the-box thinkers. These individuals are *critical* to your success. Train them how to manage—and train—those under them. Even then, you may need to micro-monitor until they are ready to steer the ship no matter which way the winds blow.

CHAPTER 6
POWER DISTANCE: HIGH VS. LOW

On August 6, 1997, a Korean Air Boeing 747 crashed into a hill on approach to the international airport in Guam, killing 228 of the 254 people aboard.

Tragically, the accident was an avoidable one. The copilot and flight engineer knew they were flying dangerously, but never confronted the captain. Captains at Korean Air were like gods—and the copilot and flight engineer could not directly confront the "god's" mistakes. In essence, they allowed the plane to crash, rather than rupture the culture and overcome the "power distance."

Geert Hofstede defines power distance as, "the extent to which the less powerful members of institutions and organizations within a country expect and accept that power is distributed unequally."[29]

---

29. Hofstede, *Culture's Consequences*, 98.

In *High* Power Distance cultures, those in less powerful positions accept that they are less powerful and essentially cannot (or will not) do anything to close the distance. North Korea or Iraq under Saddam Hussein would be examples of High Power Distance societies. There, the most powerful leaders are seen as supreme and untouchable. Citizens below accept this arrangement or die.

In *Low* Power Distance cultures, people embrace a deep sense of human equality and believe that what power distance is there should be minimized. Some of the clearest examples are Scandinavian cultures where equality is actively sought after and built into the system. Leaders and bosses are expected to consult and listen to those under them. Those in lower positions expect equality and the possibility of rising to positions of leadership and influence.

What is the acceptable—and expected—difference in power between two levels of society or two job title levels? If the power distance is large, then the lower level is expected to serve the higher level without asking questions or expecting gratitude or reward. This is not the case if the power distance is low.

Power distance is strongly correlated with the Relationship Cultural Dimension. Those cultures on the far Community end of the Relationship continuum almost always have much higher power distance than those from the Individual side of the line. Therefore, most Honor/Shame and Power/Fear cultures exhibit High Power Distance.

Power distance is a relatively new concept and so may be unfamiliar to some readers. The table below contrasts the characteristics of High and Low Power Distance cultures. You will be able to quickly identify where you and your culture lie on the spectrum between High and Low Power Distance.

POWER DISTANCE CHARACTERISTICS

HIGH Power Distance

1. Expected to show proper respect for those more powerful
2. Decisions are not questioned by those in lower positions
3. Patronage is practiced by those at the top and expected by those at the bottom
4. Responsibility is passed up the hierarchy
5. Subordinates expect to be told what to do
6. Hierarchy and power structures are rigid

7. Elders (parents and other older individuals) are respected and feared
8. Power inequalities are just a fact of life; everyone has a specific or rightful place in the power structure

LOW Power Distance

1. General disregard for hierarchy and discomfort with inequalities
2. Questioning of decisions is acceptable and even expected
3. Each person looks after herself and her horizontal community
4. Responsibility is taken personally
5. Subordinates expect to be part of decision making
6. Hierarchy and power structures are functional, not culturally assigned, and are therefore changeable and adaptable
7. Respect is given based on merit and accomplishment
8. Power inequalities are not—or should not be—set in stone

How high or low is the power distance in your own culture? How high or low is it in the culture in which you work or plan to invest?

Power Distance[30]

---

30. Informed by "Compare countries." Hofstede Insights. Accessed December 12, 2017. https://geert-hofstede.com/countries.html and personal experience.

UNPACKING POWER DISTANCE: HIGH VS. LOW

Power distance is typically one of the biggest differences between the West and most other cultures. Many Western readers of this book will come from a Low Power Distance culture, so I'll concentrate on unpacking the less familiar high end of the Power Distance cultural belief system.

High Power Distance is not bad in and of itself. It does, however, pose challenges for progressive, growth-oriented businesses. It will almost certainly drive many Western managers to distraction, if not understood and shaped.

You are not going to completely close the power distance—that's not a useful goal. Be realistic in your expectations. After each belief below, we will lay out the behaviors that result from the belief and then give a few tips on how to leverage the strengths of High Power Distance and mitigate the weaknesses.

BELIEF 1: POWER INEQUALITIES ARE JUST A FACT OF LIFE; EVERYONE HAS A SPECIFIC OR RIGHTFUL PLACE IN THE POWER STRUCTURE AND THIS HIERARCHY IS RIGID.

Power hierarchies are perceived as set in stone. Upward mobility is rare. No amount of effort, initiative, or good performance is likely to shift power dynamics, some of which have played out over centuries.

This belief differs for those who have the power and those who do not, and the behaviors and responses for both are different. I will deal with them separately under the "haves" and the "have nots."

BUSINESS BEHAVIORS OF THOSE WHO *HAVE* POWER:

Behavior: Those who have power seek to hoard it; authority is rarely delegated.

In High Power Distance cultures, those in positions of authority actively protect their power and position by ensuring that all significant decisions, and even most inconsequential ones, pass through them; authority is rarely delegated.

In these cultures, the only signature that counts is the top dog's. I tried to lease a 10 meter by 15 meter piece of land that belonged to a police district in Kabul for an antenna site. We are talking about a $300 per month expense. For this lease, I had to get the signature of the country's minister of interior! That was at least six layers of responsibility up from where it would have been signed in the West.

Pushing authority and responsibility downward is seen as losing power and, in a zero-sum world, losing power is akin to signing your own death warrant. We will cover this in more detail in Chapter 10: Zero-Sum Mindset.

Behavior: Businesses become synonymous with their owners or patrons, which can lead to catastrophic failure when these owner/patrons leave.

It is inevitable that owners and CEOs in High Power Distance cultures become the face of the company. This happens often even in Medium Power Distance countries like the U.S. (In contrast, how many "rock star" CEOs are there in Nordic countries?).

However, with authority and responsibility concentrated at the very top, many frontier market companies are vulnerable to collapse if the owner or CEO dies or resigns. Leadership capacity within the company tends to be very shallow. Very little practical leadership development and few opportunities for leadership practice cascade down.

INVESTOR TIP

When looking at a business for investment purposes, dig "behind the veil" until you find the real power, which could rest with an elder or warlord behind the scenes. Then carefully analyze the power structure within the company. Proceed with caution if the power distance is very high and seems unlikely to shift.

EFFECTIVE RESPONSES TO THOSE WHO *HAVE* POWER:

Response: Identify the subtle ways that High Power Distance is reinforced through the company and modify it where it is detrimental to business.

Examine your own business or organization to see where High Power Distance is practiced. Do managers lord it over people reporting to them? Do men shut down women's voices? Do elders expect unquestioning obedience? In most High Power Distance cultures, removing power distance completely is both not possible and not advantageous to the business, but there will be places in your company where the High Power Distance will be detrimental.

In the case of Korean Air, junior officers were expected to iron captains' uniforms, which helped maintained the High Power Distance. After the Guam crash, the airline finally recognized the problem of the power distance, and analyzed every tradition, training, and operating procedure to see where the gulf between superiors and subordinates was widest. As a consequence, they cut out certain practices that preserved power distances, including junior officers ironing captains' uniforms.

Shifting power distance is a challenge, so be prepared to pick your battles. Still, you can find ways to eliminate or at least roll back certain traditions or procedures that hold the company back. Pay attention to keeping your own power distance low and displaying this in a multitude of ways. Point out the benefits to the company when every voice is heard and every human resource is used. Seeing you reward and honor those who treat others as equals will go a long way in changing the culture in the company as a whole.

Response: Instill vision.

Vision is the most powerful belief shifter. You hold a belief because it works for you. Power distance is a belief. If High Power Distance has worked for the leader up to this point, the only way that belief will shift is to come to the conclusion that it won't lead to where they want to go in the future—that it won't lead to their vision.

If the leader comes to believe that High Power Distance is detrimental to the business and therefore to them, it will change. But you cannot dictate a shift from the outside; it must come from within. Enroll the powerful person into a vision that power is not zero sum, but additive (see Chapter 10: Zero-Sum Mindset). It may take you proving it over time, but it is worth the journey. Behaviors do not change unless beliefs change.

Response: Create a leadership or management team and endow it with the necessary authority to make decisions and develop leaders to be part of that team.

Don't try to immediately devolve power to the lowest rungs of the ladder. It is too big of a shock to the system. Anytime you modify the power structure, the participants may see it as dangerous to themselves. Before you look to results, you'll need to start with a mindset shift.

One way to begin to shrink power distance is to create a leadership or management team under the CEO/owner with real power and authority. You may be surprised at how often this doesn't exist or exists only on paper. Getting CEOs or owners to devolve power is often met with resistance, but making smaller steps can be more palatable to the powers that be. The key is to show how decreasing the power distance enhances the standing of the company and therefore the standing of the CEO/owner. Invite people at much lower levels to participate in decision-making bodies and monitor to see that this happens across the company. Positive results will begin to shift the zero-sum view of power.

At Roshan, I invited every employee who had any supervisory responsibilities (even if it was in name only) to be part of my daily morning status meeting. Each would give the status and plans for his or her area. By culture, there would have been a natural hierarchy based on position, age, or social status, and only a group of three or four "senior" members would have met with the boss. But by inviting people farther down the chain, I set the tone for a diminished power distance.

Invest in leadership development from top to bottom and monitor and reward the delegation of power. Do not train in simple leadership principles; these are too often simply memorized and never implemented. Instead, find leadership training that engages at the belief and mindset level and opens up the space for participants to see where their leadership beliefs are and are not working to get them to their personal vision[31].

This leadership development is actually the first step in succession planning. Official succession planning—other than in a family business—is often seen as threatening and therefore must be eased in. If new, capable leaders are being trained up, succession planning become more naturally part of doing business.

BUSINESS BEHAVIOR OF THOSE WHO *DO NOT* HAVE POWER:

Behavior: Responsibility is passed up the hierarchy.
Subordinates, even senior ones, wait to be told what to do and actively resist taking responsibility or showing initiative.

Taking responsibility and initiative can be a real challenge for companies in High Power Distance cultures. Subordinates, even relatively senior ones, will often wait to be told what their task is before beginning any work. For certain tasks and especially in emergencies, this can be highly effective. More often, however, it results in serious inefficiencies and undermines efforts to build a complex, multi-layered business.

Employees often resist responsibility because they feel they do not have the power or authority to make decisions anyway. There can be a sense of helplessness by those in lower power positions; they can feel powerless to achieve the desired results.

In the lease-signing story above, a number of beliefs and mindsets are at play, all related to the wide chasm between the

---

31. If you're looking for leadership development that brings effective and practical change, I give my highest recommendation to Jean Jobs, founder of YellowMarker (www.yellowmarker.com). She has trained leaders in numerous different cultural settings around the world, including multiple groups of leaders for my companies in Afghanistan.

power of the lowest and highest rungs of the ladder. If a senior leader, still below the level of Minister of Interior, took the initiative to sign my petition, not only might he be shamed or punished if it was a mistake, but the powers above him might have thought he was making a power play—which could be fatal. In a High Power Distance culture, it's not even within most people's realm of possibility to take the responsibility by signing.

In addition, when failures do occur, High Power Distance cultures allow neatly for blame to be distributed to the "other."

The dynamics are somewhat analogous to the hierarchical structures of Western militaries. The "grunt" at the bottom of the ladder waits for an order and then executes it. For certain tasks, this is highly effective, but for running innovative, nimble companies, it becomes an impediment. Special Operations soldiers are far closer to the ideal. Yes, orders come down from above, but there is significant freedom in planning and execution of the plan.

EFFECTIVE RESPONSES TO THOSE WHO DO NOT HAVE POWER:

Response: Enroll those with less power in a new vision.

Behavior follows belief and belief is shifted through new vision.

Vision creates a space for growth and progress, as I have stated before. Paint the big picture and explain to your entrepreneurs and employees why they are important in getting to that destination. Bring their personal visions out on the table and find ways to align their personal vision with the company's. This is not a once-and-done step, but an iterative process. In most cases, people will be skeptical because they have never been asked to be part of a larger vision.

By working through this process, you are enrolling them in the company vision and giving them ownership of it. This will often be new to them. It will not only motivate them to give their all, but also lessen the power distance gap between you. As they see their unique contribution to attaining the vision, it empowers them.

Response: Give responsibility and authority to your staff and don't allow them to give it back.

There is no better way to decrease power distance than to simply give responsibility and authority to those below you. The challenge will come in not taking it back when they try to hand it back. Be ready to dig for the belief that underlies their need to abdicate. Are they afraid of failure? Do they not know how to tell you that the project is off track or ill-conceived? Is there an older employee who stands in their way and they don't know how to get around the obstacle with honor maintained? Probe, but do not relent.

Response: Make sure that anytime someone says "yes" to a request, they know they will be held responsible and monitored. Then check in frequently to ensure they are on the right track.

You must assume that a "yes" to any request is always suspect, until you've significantly decreased the power distance of your company generally or have at least decreased it with those reporting directly to you. You're going to continue to get a lot of inaccurate "yeses" as long as people equate shame with saying "no." You must come up with a verification process to know if "yes" means "yes," not "maybe" or "no."

First, make sure those you are dealing with understand your English, but remember you're in their country, so be gentle. You can quickly learn to simplify your vocabulary and speak a bit more slowly (but not more loudly!). You'll also come to understand the English proficiency of each person. For important instructions, have them repeat what you've just said.

Second, confirm that they understand and are ready to proceed by having them talk through the first steps they'll take, who or what they need as resources, and what is the expected result. Remember, you're not talking to children, just making sure you haven't put them into a position where they fear that they will be shamed in some way.

Third, reiterate and have them agree to the fact that they will be held responsible for the results.

Finally, monitor their initial progress quickly so you're sure they've gotten a good start (see micro-monitoring on page 137).

Response: Show respect downward; communicate to the entrepreneurs you are investing in and to your staff that you are here to help them grow. Build trust through relationships.

Those at the top in High Power Distance cultures are often not committed to helping those below grow into their full potential. Of course, the patronage model that takes care of the physical needs of those below is commendable, but it rarely includes helping them realize their full potential (see Belief 3 below). When you genuinely deal with people as valuable and as worthy of your investment, the returns will be enormous.

One way to show real individual care while maintaining a healthy power distance is to say, "I will help make you successful and reach your vision." In other words, "I have the power to help you *and* I care about your individual success."

Use whatever relationship-building rituals are appropriate (and the time needed) to deepen relationships with your investees and employees. Relationship and connection shrink the power distance.

If your employees trust that you have their best interests in mind and that you truly want to decrease the power distance, they will be more willing to challenge your ideas and decisions and take initiative and responsibility.

A CAVEAT: DON'T DANCE WITH THE BOYS!

Destageer and I were at an Afghan wedding. It was the usual community-wide party, with huge trays of food and lots of dancing—all segregated male/female, of course. Many of my employees were there and were having a grand time trying to best each other dancing traditional Afghan dances. They tried to get me out on the dance floor, too.

I thought it would be a great opportunity to connect with my employees, but Destageer stopped me. "Don't dance with the boys," he said. His point was that I needed to be cautious about closing the power distance too much, lest I lose the necessary authority and respect needed to run a company in these traditional Community and Honor/Shame cultures. In subsequent weddings, I did hit the dance floor, but I always kept Destageer's words in mind as I interacted with my employees on and off the dance floor. It is such a balancing act between lifting up those below you and not losing the necessary authority of your place as the leader in a hierarchical and High Power Distance culture.

BELIEF 2: THOSE WITH POWER, ESPECIALLY ELDERS, ARE TO BE RESPECTED AND FEARED.

Age is one of the strongest indicators of power or influence in High Power Distance cultures. There is a rich respect for their elders that is often missing in Western countries. If those in apparent power are not the oldest, their source of power usually ties back to someone who is older.

But at its most fundamental, it is the person with *perceived* power who has the power, whether their power base would stand up to any real scrutiny or not. When the cultural default is to accept power structures as is and simply find your place within it, a person in a High Power Distance culture doesn't usually challenge the apparent status quo. Fear is imbedded in any power differential and that fear keeps the differential intact, whether coming from founding directors, a wealthy patron, or the "godfather." Their position is not commonly challenged.

Behavior: People will rarely disagree with or challenge elders or those in authority.

People will almost always say "yes" to someone in authority and will not challenge your requests or directions, especially in public. This is great for your ego—and great in emergencies—but not so beneficial when growing a multi-layer or complex company or organization.

Authority, power, and responsibility reside at the top of the ladder in High Power Distance cultures and the distance from the top to the bottom is exceedingly far. Those below the top do not believe they have the right to publicly question the mandates from on high. This often leads to a muting or limiting of new ideas. It can also mean that while individuals agree in public with a particular approach or decision, they will then fail to take it forward or even actively undermine its progress.

In addition, the respect given to elders can often mean that elders within the workplace are never disagreed with or challenged. Unfortunately, in many instances, the elders are the least educated and the least progressive in their ideas. This leads to a muting of new ideas and vision.

Behavior: Rising stars within a company often seek to lord power over their new subordinates.

As individuals gain power or position within companies, they will frequently begin to exert that power—often ungracefully—over fellow employees or clients. At times, this will play out in remarkably direct or public ways: staff will grandstand or issue demands, making a show of their newfound authority. Other times, the power games will play out in far more subtle ways: offers to "help" junior staff with tasks that they are clearly capable of doing or seeking out private audiences with senior executives to share "concerns" about colleagues.

One of my employees was promoted to a more senior management position. Suddenly he started sending his former colleagues out on all kinds of errands, both business and personal. He would hold court in his office, almost as if sitting on a throne, and rain down fire on anyone who didn't acquiesce to his authority. At the same time, he would send Destageer and me reports on all the weaknesses and failures of his staff. Though we worked with him to mitigate his warlord tendencies, we were unable to shift his beliefs and behavior and eventually had to let him go.

Response: Embrace your own power.

Stay conscious of your position of power and authority, and what it means for the validity of information that you receive. Embrace the power! There is a lot of good that can be done with it, if wielded wisely. This is particularly important for women and others who may be considered within the surrounding culture to be "weaker." Resist the urge to be overly humble or too familiar, particularly at the beginning. Within High Power Distance cultures, you need power to succeed.

Response: Ask those in positions of power to solicit new ideas from younger employees.

Those in positions of power or authority in your company, especially elders, can be "gatekeepers" for more junior employees, who are reluctant to share their ideas. If you enroll someone more powerful in this very important task, you'll be surprised by the quality and quantity of new ideas that might come up.

Ask those with power to lead brainstorming sessions. Be clear that the task is to elicit new ideas, even seemingly crazy ones, and that they will need to resist guiding the discussion or inserting their own ideas. Old habits die hard, so you may need to monitor this until everyone gets the hang of it. This practice will go a long way in modeling a smaller power distance.

Response: Rarely, if ever, publicly disagree with or directly challenge an older employee; sideline their less constructive ideas softly and quietly.

This is not to say in any way that older employees do not have great ideas. However, as with any person, some ideas are good and some not so good, and it can be challenging to disagree with or counter the not so good ideas of elders. The mandate to respect elders is so strong that employees may turn against you if you directly and publicly challenge an older person. They will do so even if they think you're right.

At times, the way to go about it is to simply acknowledge and then ignore bad or old ideas coming from elders. Hear them out in public, thank them for their ideas, and then move on. If they continue to advocate for their ideas, make sure you are not missing anything in their proposal, and then speak with them privately about why their idea will not work for the company.

Response: Act quickly, but gently, when those in power within the company overstep or lord their authority over others.

It is important that this "lording over" is gently—and privately—dealt with and not allowed to continue. Assume that they are simply acting out of the "tradition" of power and not with a mean spirit. Explore the belief or mindset that underlies the behavior. Is it a zero-sum view of power (see Chapter 10: Zero-Sum Mindset)? Is it the Survival Mindset that leads to hoarding of power (see Chapter 11: Survival Mindset)?

If the person overstepping authority is older, take them aside and enroll them in their responsibilities of raising up the younger generation. An older employee who is switched on is a very powerful ingredient for you and your company's success, due to the power and respect that such a person wields. Sometimes, though, they will have risen to a high position simply because of their age or longevity of service. They may seek to exert their power where they neither have the authority nor the expertise. If they are not able to shift, it may mean moving the person into a position with an honorable title, but with little real power or responsibility. Whatever you do, do so gently and with respect.

BELIEF 3: PATRONAGE IS EXPECTED BY THOSE AT THE BOTTOM AND PRACTICED BY THOSE AT THE TOP.

The concept of patronage is one that could take a whole chapter to unpack, but suffice it to say that patronage is the expectation that those in higher power positions will take care of those in lower positions in exchange for respect and honor.

The U.S. could, of course, learn a few things from this patronage model. Too many business owners and bosses in the U.S. have become disengaged from the welfare of those at the bottom. Paying a salary becomes merely a financial transaction; I give you money, you give me work. Work-life balance is of no concern. And loyalty becomes a rarer and rarer response.

Behavior: Those in lower levels of power expect you to solve their and their family's physical needs.

Work and private life intermingle far more in Community-oriented and High Power Distance cultures than they do in most Western cultures. You will be brought into more personal and family issues than you are likely used to and you will be expected to assist in some solutions. It may seem that this expected patronage model is a contradiction to the general attempt to lessen the power distance, but this is one place where the benefits of maintaining a sometimes detrimental cultural practice are stronger than the potential downsides.

Response: Be ready to be involved in your employees' personal and family lives.

Take care of your employees. Know what is going on in their personal lives. Crucially, know the health of their parents; sick parents will often distract them more than even sick children.

Set up clear and transparent rules about who is considered family and therefore whose sickness or funeral entitles them to leave—and specify how many days of leave. The definition of family in many countries includes their uncle's sister-in-law's brother's nephew or their third cousin twice removed (seriously). It makes for grand weddings and a certain amount of social safety net, but it can wreak havoc on sick and bereavement leave policies if you define family in their broad terms.

Set up some type of catastrophic health insurance, at a minimum, if it is available. Create an individual health savings fund that employees can dip into for normal health expenses. It doesn't have to be a huge expense. Unfortunately, government health plans are either nonexistent in most frontier markets or force people to low-quality hospitals and doctors.

Many times, the simple act of showing genuine interest in them and in their family's lives is all that is needed. These investments of time and money in your employees will pay you back many times over.

CHAPTER 7

COMMUNICATION: DIRECT VS. INDIRECT

An Afghan proverb says, "Speak to the door and the wall will hear."

Our Afghan business partner at Silk Road Solutions came to Susan's and my office one day. He started on a long and winding story that seemed to circle around and around without any apparent point and no clear subject. We'd worked together long enough that we generally got to the point quickly, but this time he was not getting there at all. Susan and I began probing, but to no avail. After at least forty-five minutes, he seemed to begin to narrow into one subject, but with multiple hems and haws. Finally, he blurted out that he needed a loan.

Western cultures tend to be far more direct in their communication styles than other cultures. We celebrate those among us who speak their minds openly and frankly. In Indirect cultures, that frankness is often regarded as appalling and very shameful.

When I was brainstorming for this book with my Afghan colleagues and employees, the topic of direct vs. indirect communication consistently came to the forefront as one of the most important concepts to understand for managing cross-culturally. Everyone had countless disaster stories about expats who either didn't understand this concept or didn't care and caused irreparable damage.

The concept of indirect communication is closely tied to the Honor/Shame Worldview, but finds its way into most cultures outside of the West. Interestingly enough, being married to a Brit and having numerous British friends, I have found—sometimes painfully—that Brits are significantly less direct than Americans. (I've also found that the Dutch are far more direct than even Americans!)

Communication[32]

UNPACKING COMMUNICATION: DIRECT VS. INDIRECT

Let's walk through three beliefs, the five resultant behaviors, and the six necessary, effective responses for Direct vs. Indirect Communication.

---

32. Approximate, based on Hall, Edward T. Beyond Culture. New York: Anchor Books, 1989.

BELIEF 1: COMMUNICATION IS MORE ABOUT RELATIONSHIPS THAN INFORMATION.

Most people would agree that rich and meaningful communication has a relationship at its foundation. Too often in the West, however, communication has become simply sharing of data or information. This problem is rarely the case in Indirect Communication cultures. These cultures are keenly aware of how your words affect the relationships that are involved or represented in the communication (e.g., their communities).

Behavior: Communication takes time.

If communication depends on relationships, then it is no wonder communication takes time and effort to develop. You will spend more time than you are used to getting to know people before any business takes place.

Response: Start from the indirect and work toward the direct.

Never start with the direct. This principle is an overarching one. Take the time to reinforce the relationship. Honor the person (find something!) before getting to the point. Start with indirect and move to direct. If you're giving a correction, perhaps start by using the word "we" or "all of us", as in, "All of us need to remember to do it this way" or "We need to get better at this task." Then drill down to the specific correction, action, or task needed and the desired expectation or result. You may never need to say, "You need to change this," but the individual will understand without feeling shamed.

BELIEF 2: INDIRECT COMMUNICATION IS A DANCE WITH THE MUSIC BEING HONOR AND COMMUNITY.

Direct communication is like taking an axe to a tree. The purpose is clear; the sharper the edge of the axe, the more quickly it is accomplished. Indirect communication is much more like a dance. You move, I move, we circle the dance floor. The dancers move and sway to the tune of their context: honor, relationship, and community. There may or may not be a clear destination, but either way you never get there in a straight line.

Behavior: Some conversations can wander round and round, looping back on themselves with no clear theme.

Turn up the sensitivity on your cultural antenna to high, if you ever find yourself in a conversation with a colleague or employee that wanders all over the place without any evident purpose. Look for the indirect message he or she is sending. It may be within the wandering conversation. It may be waiting to be asked about. Or it may come at the very end.

Behavior: Requests, especially personal requests, often come to you through a third person.

Don't be surprised when someone approaches you with a request that is actually from a third person. I find this happens often with requests for vacation or bereavement leave (a too common occurrence in most frontier markets). It can also happen with requests for raises or promotions. It is usually part of the Honor/Shame paradigm that is so often connected to the Indirect Communication Dimension. The person requesting something may feel it is shameful to make the request directly. In addition, it may not always be clear who the request is for.

Response: Become practiced at hearing and giving indirect messages.

You need to become good at picking up the indirect messages being sent to you. There are a number of ways to discern indirect messages.

When conversations or discussions seem to meander, circle around or repeat themselves, chances are an indirect message is being sent.

When you are being told a story about someone else's behavior who you are not directly connected to, know that it may actually be meant for you. People may be trying to communicate something important to you about your behavior without shaming you. This can happen when you've committed a cultural faux pas and people want to try to helpfully correct you without being the messenger of shame.

Response: Don't get impatient when requests come to you through a third person.

It's easy to snap at the messenger, "Tell them to come themselves!", but until you've established a company culture where employees believe these requests are not shameful, I encourage you to be gentle. When a person seems to be the mouthpiece for someone else, try to understand who is behind the message. Say to them, "I'd be happy to discuss this with whomever you're representing [or the person's name if you know who the requestor is]."

BELIEF 3: YOUR FUNDAMENTAL RESPONSIBILITY IN COMMUNICATION IS TO MAINTAIN THE HONOR OF BOTH PARTIES.

Indirect cultures are almost always either predominately Honor/Shame or have a strong component of it. Communication, therefore, is structured around or enveloped in the constant conversation about maintaining honor and avoiding shame.

Behavior: Bad news is alluded to, talked around, or simply not shared.

I pointed out previously that bad news is not shared readily because of the shame it is thought to bring. Sometimes, however, it is brought to light, but not in a form that we immediately understand.

Numerous times when we were just ready to sign a lease for a new office or antenna site, my site deployment person would suddenly say, "I think we should look in another area." Why would we look in another area when we're just ready to sign for this property? Often, this meant they couldn't bring themselves to say directly that the owner had backed out of the negotiated lease.

The Indirect culture believes that the shame of bad news doesn't really "stick" if it is shared obliquely, circuitously, or tangentially.

Behavior: When you've offended someone, you may never know about it directly.

When offended, an individual in an Indirect culture will tend to lick his or her wounds rather than go for a frontal attack. A mitigating factor is that most Indirect cultures are also Community cultures, and therefore the wound is shared with the community. If you have good, trusted connections into the community or within your workplace, you can continually monitor what wounds have been inflicted by checking in with them periodically. To your face, though, there may be no indication at all.

Response: Accept that correcting someone can be time consuming because it has to be done in private and with many words.

A person from a Direct Communication culture usually loves to air things out immediately, deal with problems, and then get on with work. This doesn't work in an Indirect culture.

It will take real discipline to bite your tongue in *public* and take the time to deal with things in *private*. However, even in private, you may inadvertently administer shame if you go in immediately and directly. Depending on the trust and length of your relationship, you may need to compliment, honor, and talk about the weather before coming to the point.

Become practiced at saying, "How might we do this better?", rather than, "This is not the right way!" "Do you see any other possibilities?" is a way to tell them indirectly that the way it is being done now is not correct. It might seem like a waste of time and words, but often a simple rephrasing can make your words bring action or change rather than defensiveness and shame.

Response: Do not publicly reprimand anyone. If someone needs correcting, make a broad statement about the problem (e.g., lateness), even if everyone knows it is directed toward an individual.

Be discerning in when and how you communicate directly. Rarely, if ever, correct someone or point out anything negative about them in front of a group. (I recommend not doing this at all until you are deeply knowledgeable about the far-reaching repercussions of public criticism in the operating culture.) Misbehavior is shameful and an individual who is called out publicly will go into fight-or-flight mode without really hearing even constructive criticism. If a behavior needs to be corrected, speak publicly about the behavior, using general terms, without making it obvious who the culprit is. Better yet, confront or give constructive criticism privately.

Response: Always be aware of the potential for shame when asking for status reports.

As I mentioned above, practice listening for indirect messages. In the case of status reports, whether formal or informal, accept that there very likely will be an avoidance of reporting bad news and you will need to read between the lines. If you are aware of this potential for shame, you can probe from multiple directions to get to the important information. Ultimately, creating an environment where bad news is good news should be the goal, as I described on pages 68 and 78.

CHAPTER 8

PRODUCTIVITY: PEOPLE VS. TASKS AND TIME

During the early days of Roshan, we needed to install a mobile phone antenna site on the road from Jalalabad to the Pakistan border. The area was under the nominal control of the Afghan government, but the real power rested with a powerful and often brutal local Pashtun commander who had twelve sons and innumerable grandsons and nephews.

An Afghan and an Indian engineer went to the district, rented a site from a poor landowner, and began work on the new antenna site. Three days before the on-air date Roshan had promised the provincial governor, the commander drove up to the site, closed down all work, dismantled the antenna, and arrested all the workers.

Destageer and Steve, an expat executive, were called for help. Everyone warned Destageer to stay away. They were sure that he and Steve would be beaten if they showed up. But

Destageer understood the culture and what had been missed and headed out to address the problem.

Destageer and Steve were initially rebuffed when they arrived at the commander's compound, but were eventually led to a guest meeting room. The commander appeared with two of his sons, who were holding AK-47s. Up to this point neither Destageer nor Steve had been offered the obligatory tea. Destageer knew it was not by accident, so when the commander brusquely asked him what he wanted, he said, "I would like some tea." It was a bold move! Destageer knew, however, that tea—or lack thereof—had been the problem from the very beginning of the project. He was here to rectify that.

When the tea was brought, Destageer told Steve (in English) not to drink a drop. It is an insult in Pashtun culture to ask for tea and then not drink it and the commander asked Destageer, a Pashtun himself, why he wasn't drinking. Destageer replied that he wouldn't drink until the commander listened to them. The commander, understanding that Destageer meant to petition him respectfully, said he would listen and solve any problem Destageer had.

Destageer began with a long introduction and then mentioned that he had worked with a man named Attaullah in Ghazni. "That's my nephew," the commander exclaimed. "If you had just mentioned from the beginning that you knew Attaullah, I would have solved the problem immediately."

Destageer knew that this pre-calculated connection simply gave him credibility and a foundation for solving the problem. It took another two hours of drinking tea and discussions before the commander agreed to not only let this site go forward, but also guaranteed all other sites in the districts he controlled.

This problem never would have risen to a crisis level if the original engineers had drunk tea at the commander's house to build the foundation of relationship and honor from the start.

In the West, efficiency is king, time is money, and productivity is paramount. It is all about getting it done faster, better, and less expensively. In other cultures, relationship is king, people are more important than tasks, and efficiency takes second place to everyone feeling honored and respected. They go deep now to grease the wheels for later.

Growing up in Indonesia, I often heard the term *jam karet,* loosely translated as "elastic time." This was often used in reference to events, which often ran "late" by our Western understanding of priorities. But in Indonesia, making sure an event took place was the ultimate goal, not starting on time. Since people are the focus of the culture, it wasn't a real event until all of the people showed up.

We can all agree that both approaches have their merits. How then do we reconcile the polarities of productivity? Many of you reading this book come from the Task and Time side of the Productivity Belief. You will need help working in a setting where the People side dominates, so we'll concentrate on unpacking that next.

Productivity has a direct impact on the bottom line of a business, whether it is finalizing a deal in a timely manner or operating a business efficiently. How then do you balance the two ends of the spectrum and succeed? How do you find the strengths of each end of the spectrum and harness them for successful businesses? The starting point is gaining insight into this critical set of beliefs.

Productivity[33]

UNPACKING PRODUCTIVITY: PEOPLE VS. TASKS AND TIME

On the People side of the Productivity spectrum, we will explore three beliefs, five behaviors, and five effective responses. As all are very much interconnected, we'll do it a little differently this time and address them together by category. You have seen the core of these beliefs before, but here we will look at them in light of how they drive the People vs. Tasks and Time dynamics.

Remember, we see the behavior or action, but often do not see the underlying belief. We respond to the behavior based on *our* belief about that behavior. Until we can understand *their* belief, we will be responding to the wrong thing and will not get the results we are looking for.

BELIEF 1: RELATIONSHIPS ARE MORE IMPORTANT THAN TASKS.

Most Innocence/Guilt cultures are on the Task and Time end of the spectrum and find much of their identity in "doing," in accomplishments and money earned. Honor/Shame and Power/Fear cultures are usually on the other end of the spectrum

---

33. Approximate, based on personal experience and on Richard Lewis. (http://blog.crossculture.com/crossculture/2013/01/monochromatic-and-polychromatic-cultures.html)

and find much of their identity in "being," in community and in reputation or position.

If your identity is in relationships, then that is what you emphasize. That, by its nature, takes significant amounts of time.

BELIEF 2: RELATIONAL CONNECTIONS ARE THE FUNDAMENTAL BUILDING BLOCKS AND CURRENCY OF LIFE.

If relationships are king, then all else is built on the connections between human beings. Who you are, how you provide for your family, and how high up the ladder you go in life are all dependent on cultivating relationships with influential and powerful people.

BELIEF 3: HONOR SECURES ITS VALUE PRIMARILY THROUGH RELATIONSHIPS, RATHER THAN FROM MONEY OR ACCOMPLISHMENTS.

Honor is intrinsically connected to relationship rather than primarily money, accomplishments, or the completion of a task. Therefore, since honor is life itself, relationships will trump tasks.

Behavior: Business deals take time in the beginning.

Think of business deals as a marriage; there is lots of time spent in the dating phase before you seal the deal. Westerners too often want the "benefits" of marriage without the time and toil of relationship building. People cultures see your impatience as demeaning of them as humans. Relationships are what matter in life, not mere accomplishments and activity.

Your partners in frontier and emerging markets plan to do business with you for a long time, not just for this transaction. They take the time to establish the trust needed to move forward.

Westerners, on the other hand, want to get down to business immediately. We are used to having a system of contracts, courts and law enforcement that generally guarantee that trust is kept. The only—or at least the main—system for ensuring deals in many of the countries you will work in is the system of relationships and trust you build.

> The relationships and trust you
> build are the only system for
> ensuring deals in many countries.

Behavior: We bring our lawyers and accountants to the deal table; frontier market businesspeople bring their relatives and powerful friends.

In the West, we are generally more data- and contract-driven than relationship-driven. I often saw this thinking conflict with relationship-driven deal-making in Afghanistan. The expat lawyers for Roshan demanded multi-paged contract documents with clause after clause of CYA verbiage as a consequence of their Innocence/Guilt culture, whereas my Afghan partners wanted one page. Only one page was needed, if the relationship was there; anything more was taken as distrustful and disrespectful. If the relationship wasn't there, the contract wasn't worth the paper it was written on.

INVESTOR TIP

Never trust the piece of paper! Contractual compliance is a multi-faceted beast. Just as all cultures are a mixture of the three worldviews, so your remedy for compliance must take pieces from each.

In Honor/Shame cultures, use strong relationships to tie compliance to honor and non-compliance to shame, but indirectly communicate the consequences (i.e., seed a little fear). In Power/Fear cultures, you better have power or be aligned with someone with power, but also make the agreement very public and tie it to the position and authority (standing) of the other party. In Innocence/Guilt cultures, lawyer up and put every detail on paper!

In all cases, be creative. One way we reconciled different cultural beliefs of trust and agreement was to build in multiple and early steps of compliance, rather than one large step (such as a payment) at the end. This way you could very quickly understand if compliance would be an issue.

The challenge is that in most frontier markets there are very few, if any, neutral parties to enforce or arbitrate contract compliance. You're on your own, so build it into your risk model. And, again, never trust a piece a paper on its own.

Court systems in frontier markets are generally weak. Contract compliance relies almost exclusively on the quality of your relationship with the other party (including the power relationship) and the shame that would come from not keeping their word to a friend.

Behavior: Deadlines and start times don't carry gravitas.

The issue of starting meetings on time raises a strong difference of opinion among my Afghan and Nigerian colleagues and, I suspect, would in many cultures that are not time driven. On the one hand, some individuals want to concede to the culture. They argue for letting business meetings begin a few (or many) minutes late. The rest of my colleagues are adamant that for their countries to move forward, more discipline about time management is essential and the start time has to be enforced rigorously and continuously.

The tricky part to not starting on time is that it often goes hand in hand with not getting things done by the deadline. That, of course, can be deadly for businesses.

One of my expat friends tells a typical story of a non-Time-and-Task oriented culture: "I received twenty pages of a master's thesis from someone to edit at 8:30 p.m. When I asked when it was due, they said tomorrow! They had known about the deadline for months. It suddenly becomes *my* emergency."

This is different from the cramming and last-minute work that takes place in much of the West. Cramming almost always starts with an understanding of the amount of time needed to finish a task, but a person may not be disciplined enough to finish it before the last minute. In People cultures there is much less of a sense for how much time a task will take. The saying, "You have the watches, we have the time," reflects the sense that time is not the ticks of a metronome nor the dictates of deadlines, but the slow-moving sphere of relationships. As a result, time becomes mostly inconsequential. Their history is thousands of years old; what is a day here or there? It is a whole different way of looking at time and tasks.

Behavior: Everything takes longer.

Not only do business deals take time, but every other transaction of significance demands relationship. Relationships take time, intentionality, and long-term commitment, far more than you would expect in the West. Need I say more?

Behavior: Greetings are carried out with the utmost importance.

Think of greetings as the beginning and linchpin of every relationship. There is a protocol to greetings that must take place every single time you meet. Never, ever short-circuit the protocol.

In the West, greetings in business settings often feel almost like an afterthought. A simple "Hi" or "Hello" is acceptable in most cases, especially among friends. You get through as quickly as possible so you can get down to business. Not so in most other cultures outside the West.

In many cultures, you must ask about the other persons' family, their health, their general well-being, etc. (If you are a man, be careful about asking about their wife; in many conservative cultures it is strictly off-limits.) The funny part in Afghanistan is that the greetings on both sides many times are being said simultaneously and on top of each other. Afghans recognize this and laugh at themselves, and keep doing the exact same things. It is almost existentially important that the greeting protocol is followed.

It is important to understand greetings between sexes. Observe very carefully how your sex greets the opposite sex, including if there is a difference between how you greet a married woman and how you greet a single woman. For a man, this can mean almost the difference between life and death in some countries. Be as conservative as your colleagues in the way you greet them. Be particularly aware if you are used to shaking hands. This may be a cultural taboo in the country you are in. My rule is to not be the first person who sticks out a hand when greeting anyone I don't know.

It is also worthwhile to observe and understand *who* you greet first when you enter a room full of people of different ranks and ages. Letting your colleagues take the lead usually solves this dilemma, but, if you are forced to make a choice, remember the culture of honor and greet the person with the whitest hair first.

Practiced consistently, these responses can rescript *every* conversation you have and transform *every* relationship.

Response: Remember, "Drink tea 'til you pee!" Invest time to build relationships and it will come back many times over (we first covered this on page 88).

Western businesspeople are usually impatient when interacting with other cultures and want to launch into business discussions immediately. The antidote: drink tea (or whatever other liquid is part of relationship building). I've said it before and I'll say it again: If your bladder is not screaming, you have not spent enough time building relationships before doing business.

This is a dance. Keep in mind that your potential business partners don't Google you or look you up on LinkedIn. Instead, they drink tea with you.

Two main things are going on during the tea time. First, each side is trying to find a relational connection, figuring out if they know someone in common who can vouch for the other. Second, they're sizing up the other person for his style of doing business and negotiating, for her flexibility, etc.

You can rarely speed this process up. That being said, most of the businesspeople you are dealing with will try to use the slow pace to wear you down once negotiations start. There is always a balance that you have to strike. You will learn when the time comes to force the pace. However, that time is probably much farther out than you think. Don't be impatient. When your bladder is screaming, then it is probably about the right time to start business.

Taking time to build relationship
and trust significantly speeds up
business decisions and tasks.

The good news is that business decisions and tasks will actually speed up significantly once you have taken the extended time to build a relationship and the trust that comes with it. There are advantages to hierarchical management structures; one call will make things happen quickly when you have the trust of the big boss.

Response: Greet even the mouse.

In many countries, a relationship starts with the greeting. Take the time to learn the greeting rituals and then practice them. Know that in many cultures, this means greeting everyone!

I worked very hard at this greeting thing once I found out it was so important to Afghans. I would stop as I entered the office each day and greet each security guard personally. Every cleaner got individual attention when I would pass them in the hallways and drivers were always thanked after each ride.

But one day I got a good lesson in how you can never become complacent in greeting. I entered our open-plan office and greeted each person with a handshake—except for two of my closer Afghan colleagues, whom I hugged, as is usual among male friends in Afghanistan.

Later on that same day, I gathered everyone to do some cultural intelligence brainstorming. At the end of the time, I happened to ask them how I as their boss had not been culturally intelligent. Abdullah, one of the men who I had hugged, nailed me for a cultural faux pas.

Abdullah commented that I had shaken hands with some of the people, but hugged only him and one other. This nonequitable greeting was totally unacceptable. I looked around the room and saw a whole bunch of nodding heads. They had all noticed! It was amazing to me that there had been an instant and automatic analysis from the moment I entered the room.

Rather than get defensive or try to explain it away, I immediately apologized, jumped up, and went to each man I hadn't hugged (you definitely don't hug the women) and made sure to wrap them up in a bear hug. Honor (the employees and mine) was restored and the egalitarian greeting protocol reestablished.

Greet the housekeepers, drivers, and anyone in other "low" (as defined by the culture) positions. These greetings may not normally be done in your host culture, but it highlights your desire to develop relationships. Plus, you never know when one of these people may end up keeping you from a bad mistake or saving your life (remember my story of Naseem earlier?).

Pay attention to the little things that communicate respect and build relationships.

Response: Taking the time to build trust and respect with your employees then allows you to be more demanding on tasks and deadlines.

We've talked about building up a bank account of honor, trust, and respect with your employees. If the balance is high, you can withdraw some of it to demand speed and adherence to deadlines. When the time comes to gut it out to the finish line, employees who have been respected and trusted will respond in extraordinary ways. This is really just human nature across all cultures, but ways of depositing in the bank account may be different for each culture.

Response: Enforce deadlines.

I have to side with my Afghan colleagues who insisted that meeting deadlines was key to a successful business and a vibrant economy. Start meetings on time, enforce consequences when deadlines are not met, tie the vision of success to meeting deadlines, and have grace when the inevitable learning curve is steep.

One reminder: never shame a person publicly for being late. Remind people publicly that meetings should start on time, but don't single out an individual. They will know who they are. If necessary, pull the offender aside privately and enroll him in the need for promptness.

Response: When handling conflict, be more relationship centric than problem centric.

It is easy to immediately go into problem-solving mode when presented with a conflict. This works far better in a culture where logic and data prevail, though even there it has its limits. However, in a People (i.e., relationship) culture, you will have far more success if you clearly see and prioritize the people and relationships involved in the conflict.

The problem is not an equation to be solved, but rather a complex and nuanced dance of complex and nuanced humans. Take a deep breath and use the Belief Tool to dig for the beliefs at play in the conflict. Once you see the underlying beliefs, you can figure out a solution.

CHAPTER 9

DESTINY: FATALISM VS. PERSONAL CONTROL

During my years growing up in Indonesia, I saw people intentionally look in the opposite direction to traffic when taking the first step to cross a street. They believed that if they did not look, they were not responsible for what happened, and God would dictate the result.

This sense of fatalism is also at play in many frontier markets, including Afghanistan. Afghan fighters are famous for standing up in the middle of a firefight and simply rushing the enemy front on—one reason they have been so hard to conquer militarily. It is not that they think they have magical powers, as some historical African warriors did. Instead, they simply believe that they will die when it is their time to die, and not a moment sooner. This belief has served the country well in war, but it is one of those "winning" strategies that rarely works well in business.

Conversely, many people at the Personal Control end of the Destiny spectrum believe they can create their own destiny and future in life. This often leads to high levels of competitiveness and an over-emphasis on winning at all costs. A strong sense of personal motivation is often the result, but they can become stressed and paralyzed if they feel that life is out of control.

Fatalism is commonly part of the Honor/Shame and Power/Fear Worldviews. It is intensified when a person experiences chronic poverty and insecurity. Personal Control, by contrast, is usually a characteristic of the Innocence/Guilt Worldview, though strands of fatalism show up in countries with a Christian influence.

I'll unpack Fatalism, since it is usually quite different from the worldview of most readers.

Destiny[34]

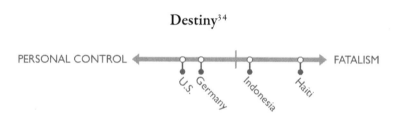

UNPACKING DESTINY: FATALISM VS. PERSONAL CONTROL

In a high Fatalism culture, you generally find the strongest fatalism at the lowest levels of a business or organization. The higher up you go, which usually means more education, more experience of control over results and more exposure to less fatalistic cultures, the more fatalism moves from the micro to the

---

34. Approximate based on World Values Survey. WVS Database. Accessed December 12, 2017. http://www.worldvaluessurvey.org/WVSOnline.jsp.)

macro. Still, you will find vestiges of it in almost any person who believes in a supreme being(s) or forces.

You will generally find the
strongest levels of fatalism at the
lower levels of your business
or organization.

BELIEF 1: I AM NOT IN CONTROL OF MY FUTURE. SUCCESS (OR FAILURE) ARE CAPRICIOUS AND ONLY LOOSELY TIED TO MY COMPETENCE, SKILL, OR EFFORT.

In fatalistic societies, the general pervasive belief is that I, as an individual, am too small and powerless to affect how my life will unfold. Success is not determined by one's effort or intelligence. Far more often it is determined by power and money. Even survival is seemingly fickle. A rocket screams into a crowded street. Two friends dive to the ground; only one stands up again. Their competence, skill, or effort made no difference to which one survived.

In many societies, fatalism is taught and reinforced from childhood. A child's place in society is set at birth based on forces over which they exercise no control: power, money, position, ethnicity, citizenship, etc. Once set, few within these cultures believe that they can be changed significantly. The caste system that still holds such significance in India is one extreme example, but the same principles of fatalism are alive and well in many other countries and communities.

*Behavior: Entrepreneurs hesitate to enter the arena and
employees may at times appear apathetic or unambitious*

Why try, if you're not in control of your future? Your personal
motivation to make the extra effort to get ahead is likely to be
diminished if you see yourself as a small piece of wood being
swept along on the river of life.

It is never quite this black and white, but you will find el-
ements of this thinking in entrepreneurs who are reluctant to
launch a business and employees who seem to underperform at
work.

Gabriele Ruiu, in her paper titled "The perverse effect of
fatalism on entrepreneurial selection"[35], shows that fatalism
adversely affects the entry of "high ability entrepreneurs" into
entrepreneurial endeavors. They believe that success is completely out of their control and therefore don't even make an
attempt at business.

Strong fatalism is also one component that leads to disengaged workers—and disengaged workers are much less pro-
ductive. Gallup, in their 2013 *State of the Global Workplace:
Employee Engagement Insights for the Business Leaders Worldwide* report, shows that "Work units in the top 25% of [worker
engagement] have significantly higher productivity, profitabil-
ity, and customer ratings, less turnover and absenteeism, and
fewer safety incidents than those in the bottom 25%."[36]

Though we in the West believe that fatalism doesn't work
in business, we also often take personal control to such excess
that we suffer far more stomach ulcers and stress-induced ill-
nesses. We take on intense responsibility for events that are ac-

---

35. Gabriele Ruiu, ("The perverse effect of fatalism on entrepreneurial selection," *Economics Bulletin*, Vol. 34, No. 2 (2014): 901-922

36. State of the Global Workplace: Employee Engagement Insights for the
Business Leaders Worldwide (2013), page 7, http://www.gallup.com/ser-
vices/178517/state-global-workplace.aspx

tually outside our control. We could do with more of a *"que sera sera"* attitude at times.

Response: Clearly connect results to efforts and then to rewards.

Fatalism is strongest in the least educated and least experienced. Demonstrate to such employees in very tangible ways that business results come from effort. Start with small results to show the connections and then move to bigger results. This may seem obvious, but some people grow up with a philosophical disconnect between the two, at least in certain arenas of life.

Tying efforts to rewards is most powerful. Don't assume you know what rewards are most valued. As in the West, rewards are often not merely monetary. Many fatalistic cultures are part of the Honor/Shame Worldview and therefore giving public honor can be a motivating reward. On the other hand, until your employees feel financially secure in their daily lives, monetary rewards will likely be most valued.

Be sure that the time between
the effort and the reward is short.

Very importantly, be sure that the time between the effort and the reward is short. If the reward is a commission, pay employees at least weekly or monthly.

Response: Show that failure is not absolute or necessarily permanent by highlighting stories of success coming out of failure.

Again, the story of the invention of the light bulb is often effective here. If Edison had stopped "failing" even one time before his final discovery, the incandescent light bulb that changed the world would not have been invented for many years.

It can be very helpful to use failure-to-success stories from the country you are in. That said, there are many examples that can connect in some frontier markets. Think about Steve Jobs being fired from Apple before he returned to make it one of the most successful and influential companies in the world; Soichiro Honda being turned down for a job at Toyota Motor Company; Michael Jordan getting cut from his high school basketball team; Bill Gates's first company failing; or Henry Ford going broke five times before finding success.

Search for and then use every opportunity to overcome even the smallest failures or setbacks in order to show that failure is not predetermined. There is no better way to show people that fatalism is not all powerful than to turn an apparent failure into a resounding success, and celebrating it publicly and loudly.

BELIEF 2: UNSEEN EXTERNAL FORCES CONSPIRE AGAINST ME.

Unseen forces—both good and evil—often play a significant role in cultures on the Fatalism end of the Destiny continuum. Fatalistic societies typically maintain deeply held beliefs in the power of good and evil forces, which must be feared, appeased, and served.

There are generally two components to these unseen forces. The first is a belief that there are all-powerful forces in the spiritual realm that control my fate and over which I have no control. The second is the belief that powerful people above me control my fate.

Though there is usually a powerful force for good in the world, unseen forces of evil are believed to actively work against one as a good person. The unseen forces are unknown and ambiguous, and all kinds of malevolent personalities are assigned to them.

Protocols and rituals must be followed and people with spiritual power or access appeased in Power/Fear cultures. This is also true of many other cultures that have a component of Power/Fear in them.

A significant portion of this comes from superstition or religion. In the Muslim world, you will very often hear, "Inshallah"—"If Allah (God) wills it."

Behavior: There is a tendency to "fail backward" rather than "fail forward."

Failure can be seen as caused by a higher power (whether in the spiritual realm or in the physical universe). Therefore, it is predetermined, rather than something to be overcome. Failure then becomes a kind of signpost from above that says, "retreat and don't try again," (i.e., fail backward instead of failing forward.) After any number of these failures, people tend to simply accept their lot in life.

Behavior: Fatalistic people tend to avoid personal responsibility, instead giving control over to external forces.

Why would you want to take responsibility for results of your efforts, if you think that you don't actually control or significantly influence them?

Response: Don't discount external forces or luck, but enroll your staff and entrepreneurs in a vision for the future.

Acknowledge belief in "fate," but get people to acknowledge that at least some things are under their control. A fisherman doesn't just sit by the river and wait for fate to send him a fish in his lap; he baits the hook and throws it in. Control what you can and leave the rest to fate. If you leave the house to go to work with no buffer for traffic and you arrive late, can you blame fate or your lack of planning? Don't let employees use fate as an excuse when it can be clearly shown that it is simply lack of preparation, planning, or competence. Remind them that they won't get to their vision if they leave everything up to some external force.

Response: If they believe in a God or gods—which most will—ask them about the expectation of personal responsibility and action demanded by that being.

Don't worry: They have much less issue talking about religion than you do. Fatalism can sometimes be used as an excuse to do nothing. It can often be couched in religious reasoning, but under polite questioning people will almost always acknowledge that the supreme being(s) they believe in demands personal responsibility and proactive action in life. Encourage them to build on that while acknowledging that there are things in life over which we do not have control.

PART IV

MINDSETS

WHY MINDSETS MATTER

As we have just seen, cultural dimensions are descriptors of the culture that a particular society has developed, often over centuries. They combine to create broader worldviews.

Mindsets, in our usage of the word, are relatively more recent experiences that have shaped a society—trauma and drama, in most cases.

Frontier markets, by definition, are those with a history of poverty, whether chronic or situational. In addition, almost without exception these areas have experienced decades of political turmoil, insecurity, ethnic strife, and/or dictatorship. Though their economies are emerging, these experiences are deeply imprinted on the people's mindsets and influence every action and attitude.

Mindsets profoundly impact investing in and growing businesses. The three mindsets we will explore—Zero-Sum, Survival, and Limited Possibilities—are "limiting" mindsets. In the chaos of war and poverty, these mindsets have worked, as evidenced by the people having survived to stand in front of you. But they will not take the country to the next level. In my experience in numerous frontier markets, these mindsets are the most limiting for business success. They must be shifted or "de-powered."

As we look at these three mindsets, remember the Belief Tool.

Every human BEHAVIOR comes out of a core BELIEF.

And the central practice:

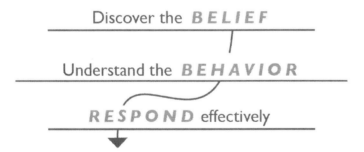

Discover the *BELIEF*

Understand the *BEHAVIOR*

RESPOND effectively

Knowing what someone believes helps us interpret their actions. Conversely, their actions can be signposts leading us to discover the underlying beliefs. In each case curiosity and humility are the prerequisites to discovery.

I find understanding these three mindsets to be particularly helpful for navigating frontier markets. They explain many of the actions you might otherwise find especially perplexing or mystifying.

CHAPTER 10
ZERO-SUM MINDSET

A zero-sum game is any game where there is always a winner and a loser, never a win-win outcome. The Zero-Sum Mindset lives in a winner/loser state of existence; the pie is always the same size and if you get some, someone else does not. It is a "scarcity" mindset, as opposed to an "abundance" mindset.

Traffic in Kabul (by Curt Laird)

Driving in Kabul is crazy. Cars jostle for every inch of room, flagrantly ignoring traffic signals (where they exist). Traffic police make feeble attempts to direct the onward surge of rubber and metal by waving their red paddles forlornly. Some succeed against all odds, but more often than not they eventually surrender to their obvious impotence and retreat to the shade.

As your car nears an intersection, you are suddenly faced with ten cars coming at you from every direction. Who is going to take the right of way? You eye the one on the left. He eyes you. You project all the Jedi power you can muster through the windshield, hoping to intimidate him. His face begins to show signs of fear. You have bested him! You step on the accelerator and then, just as quickly, slam your foot down hard on the brake. Your opponent is driving a Pakistani car with the driver on the other side. You have been jousting with the frightened passenger! The driver sails by with a condescending look on his face. Your pride lies in tatters. You slowly drive on, vowing that the next time it will be different. But it never is.

Traffic in Kabul is the perfect embodiment of a zero-sum game. An Afghan driver cannot comprehend that he would get through the intersection faster if each driver would wait their turn. In his zero-sum world, every inch of space he surrenders to another driver sets him further behind, away from his goal. Of course, as with the traffic, the results of this thinking in business mean that no one gets anywhere, at least not quickly and certainly not together.

Entrepreneurs and, in fact, any leader in these countries must shift to an abundance mindset if there is any hope of achieving the kind of private sector economic growth that will lift them out of poverty.

UNPACKING THE ZERO-SUM MINDSET

The Zero-Sum Mindset is completely understandable, if you recognize where it comes from. During times of war or sustained poverty or persecution, the pool of goods (money, resources, power) available narrows and competition rises. Those who have relatives who lived through the Great Depression in the U.S. or even the aftermath of World War II in Europe will most likely have witnessed this mindset in them. If the country where you work has experienced any trauma or poverty in its recent history, be ready to deal with this very powerful mindset.

BELIEF 1: THERE IS A FINITE AND LIMITED QUANTITY OF EVERYTHING IN LIFE: POWER, MONEY, FOOD, HONOR, ETC.

In countries with a history of conflict and poverty, the scarcity of resources during those difficult years has seeped into the everyday calculations that many of your colleagues and clients make. Long, harsh days were spent standing in winding lines to the food distribution points during those dark years of conflict. Every man, woman and child in the line knew that the UN distribution truck held only a limited amount of food, and that their family would go hungry if they didn't get to the front. Often, there was a stampede to the front when the lines opened. "Screw other families! My children need to eat!"

The Zero-Sum Mindset is prevalent even among those who did not experience the extreme drama of distribution lines. In many frontier markets, the very fact that there is not yet a thriving and healthy private sector has meant that, for most families, scarcity is the default. This applies to material resources, such as food and money, and to less tangible resources, such as power.

This belief produces two very predictable behaviors in the workplace.

Behavior: Seizure, rather than creativity.

A Zero-Sum Mindset leads to taking, rather than creating. Seizure is the only logical choice when life is lived on the assumption of scarcity and when multiplication of power and other resources is assumed to be impossible. As a result, many living in these contexts will not even ask the question of how they might create "more." Initiative and out-of-the-box thinking do not even get a start.

The Zero-Sum Mindset is one of the central reasons why so much of business activity in frontier markets is limited to simple transactions (i.e., trading or buy-low-sell-high). Entrepreneurship, by one definition, is the creation of value where there is none. When a population believes that the proverbial pie is and always will be of one size, entrepreneurship becomes far rarer.

Behavior: Warlordism in the office—hoarding power.

Warlords are the curse of Afghanistan and many other frontier and emerging markets. They may go by different names in different countries—commanders, autocrats, dictator, even just "big boss" ("*oga*" in Nigeria)—but they have the same modus operandi. Across their arena of power, they wreak havoc on those less powerful. Warlords are experts at playing the zero-sum game to their own advantage. For them, any authority they delegate is authority they lose, so they do not delegate and they do not share power.

Take warlordism into the business management arena and you have a disaster. Delegation of responsibility or authority is avoided at all costs. But it is impossible to build a business beyond a mom and pop operation without real delegation. A shift of mindset is essential.

In most frontier markets, nearly every organization is straight-line hierarchical; there is no significant decision made except by the top man (and 99.9 percent of the time it is a man). The business "warlord" may have representatives, but they exercise very little or no authority of their own. They also think very little on their own.

Over the last decade, many international training companies have sought to train frontier market businesspeople on business skills such as delegation, but have continued to see no real change to the ways in which power and authority is shared.

Over the course of a week or two, trainers will go through PowerPoints on, say, "The 21 Laws of Delegation." The management trainees, having come up through an education system that encourages rote memorization rather than critical thinking, eagerly take notes and quickly memorize every single law and every single illustration of delegation. The men and women then return to their offices, put the syllabus on the shelf, and hang their training certificate on the wall. (Afghans, especially, *love* certificates!) For all the training and certification, however, they will *never* delegate one iota.

The results of these failed training sessions will continue to be baffling until we recognize that delegation, at its core, is based on a belief that runs counter to the Zero-Sum Mindset they have operated in for years. Delegation assumes that by sharing or giving away power, you will in fact gain more power in the long run.

Decades of poverty, conflict, or political oppression, however, have convinced many around the world that delegating or sharing power is deeply dangerous, even deadly. To people in these environs, power operates on zero-sum rules. Why would you do something that you expect to bring death, or at least profound failure?

INVESTOR TIP

Look for an abundance mindset in those you intend to invest in. Are they creating or simply copying ideas, business models, or products? Is their language full of warfare or "seizure" words, even when not talking about competitors? Do they speak of collaborating and networking with existing businesses and other entrepreneurs? Quiz them on how they see the future of the country and listen for the language of possibilities, hope, and paradigm shifts.

Response: "Kill" the warlords.

You have to kill the warlords in your business. Kill them from the moment you interview your first manager candidate. Kill them when you see them order the cleaners and drivers around with a condescending attitude. Kill them by showing them that servant leadership is the best way.

Here are three ways to keep the warlords out of your business:

1. *In their first interview, get prospective employees or potential investees to acknowledge that they hate warlords—which they almost all do—and make it clear to them that there will be no warlords in your company or the companies you invest in.*

I frequently use the picture of a rising boat as an analogy to communicate the power of delegation. A boat rises as the water it rests on rises. A boat can't push down on the water to rise higher, just as a swimmer who fights the water to rise higher will quickly tire and sink below the surface. In the same way, a leader who fights the people below him to gain power eventually falls. A leader who works to raise the level of his people will rise with them, and without the churning and fighting.

2. *Relentlessly monitor your investees' and managers' relationships with their subordinates, particularly cleaners, drivers, or others in positions of low power. Draw their attention to their attitudes.*

Most of the Afghan cleaning ladies at Roshan were old enough to be my mother, so I treated them like I did my mother and they loved me for it. One day I was walking down the hall in our office and noticed the long cord of a vacuum cleaner snaking around the corner. I could hear the vacuum working vigorously in the next room. I decided I would kid around with the "auntie" on the other end of the cord. I reached down and unplugged the cord and then stood there with the end dangling in front of my face. Sure enough, I heard a long pause and then commotion.

Around the corner came a little, wrinkled old lady, scurrying to find the cause of her sudden loss of power. Her eyes were on the ground following the cord. When she looked up and saw me standing there with the plug in my hand, she broke out in the biggest smile I'd ever seen. Right there and then I had her loyalty. That I, the boss, would joke around with her, the "lowly" cleaning lady, would have made her feel tremendously respected.

From that day on, I had the cleanest office in the whole building! And still, whenever I return for a visit, the cleaning ladies come out to give me a warm welcome.

One of the most revealing behaviors that exposes the warlord heart is how a person treats those on the lowest rungs of the organization or, for that matter, of society. Notice how they interact with the cleaners and drivers or the clerks and low-level admin employees. If there is disdain or they even just ignore them, bring this to light and explore why this is happening.

3. *Model servant leadership.*

There is no better way to interrupt the zero-sum view of power than to model it through servant leadership. In many frontier markets, the concept of servant leadership is an anathema. Patronage is common, but servant leadership is not. Patronage provides for the basic physical needs of those below, but servant leadership looks at each individual and works to help them toward their personal vision. Servant leaders spend time listening and then fashion solutions and programs to the needs of the followers within the context of the business.

You, as the powerful leader, step "down" to offer your skills, knowledge, and power to those below you. I have had times when this was initially rejected by those I tried to serve because they could not wrap their heads around the boss "stooping" to their level. I would push through the resistance and explain that as one human helping another, there was no "stooping" involved.

The zero-sum view of power will not shift overnight; it is deeply embedded in their mindsets and even culture. But it pays dividends both in business success and in the success of each person you serve.

Response: Delegate authority and refuse to take it back, even when an employee no longer wants it.

Refusing to take back the responsibility or authority that you have given out is one of the most practical ways that you can model delegation. This doesn't mean that you won't have to micro-monitor, as we discussed in a previous section, but rather that you will reframe authority and responsibility for those that work with and for you.

When you have given an employee authority to undertake a task, do not let them come back to you for any kind of permission in that area. I assure you, they will try. Force them to make the decisions themselves.

We were to put up a display of Roshan's services at an exhibition in Herat. I told my team to come up with the ideas for what would be the most effective display and then execute their plan. Almost immediately they came back to me to make decisions on even small details. I sent them away empty handed. It was almost comical to see the consternation and even paralysis on their faces. These were smart, educated, capable men and women, but this was not normal for them, as they were used to the "*rais*" (i.e., boss or warlord) making all the decisions.

If employees are adamant that they cannot do something themselves, tell them you will only discuss the issue with them if they come to you with options or possible solutions. Make them do the creative thinking and problem solving themselves.

In doing so, people see that a decision that, under the hierarchical system, would be yours is now truly theirs. They also get valuable experience suggesting new, creative ways of working.

Response: Reward creativity.

The Zero-Sum Mindset and inside-the-box thinking are the opposite of creativity. Therefore, throughout the book I have encouraged you to reward creativity as an antidote to these limiting beliefs. One of the best ways to encourage creativity is to celebrate new solutions and ideas, even small ones. Find these new ideas through brainstorming. Keep sending people back to the drawing table until they have exhausted the possibilities, constantly asking them, "Is there another possibility?" Then implement the ideas and reward quickly, even before the results are in. As you reward creativity, it builds a base of evidence that diminishes the power of the Zero-Sum Mindset by demonstrating that additionality and synergy is possible.

Response: Find key creative people to show the way.

Seed the company with creative people. It will take long hours and hard work to find them, but they will be a catalyst to their cultural colleagues. Review *Response: Find outside-the-box thinkers* on page 130.

BELIEF 2: THE ONLY WAY TO GAIN MORE OF ANYTHING IS FOR SOMEBODY ELSE TO LOSE; WIN-WIN IS NOT AN OPTION.

The inevitable extension of a scarcity mindset within a zero-sum context is the belief that multiplication of resources or power is impossible. There is always a winner and a loser; there can never be a win-win situation for both parties. If *you* get two of anything, those two are taken out of *my* pie. The possibility that I might gain by helping you to also gain is nearly inconceivable.

This particular belief produces two predictable behaviors.

Behavior: Limited collaboration; hoarding information, skills, and resources.

Collaboration, by definition, is a process of give and take. If I give you my knowledge, skills, or resources and you give me yours, together they will add up to more than the components. This breaks down if each person protects what he or she has and is reluctant to throw it into the mix. Why would I share information or ideas with my coworkers if there is a limited supply and any information I give away diminishes my own stockpile of "value?"

A Zero-Sum Mindset exhibits an almost obsessive protection of personal possessions and resources. It will not take the risk of releasing resources to add to others' and create something bigger and better; synergy is not practiced.

In the early days of Roshan, there was an almost inexhaustible need for training of every type, whether technical skills or leadership and management practices. The standard training method was train the trainer, so that is what we did. But as we looked at the spread of the knowledge and skills, we saw that the vast amount of knowledge passed on to the new trainers became only a trickle when they passed it on to the next level. Was this a result of laziness? Incompetence? What was going on? The behaviors didn't make sense.

A trainer's goal in the West is to help the trainees reach the master's level in the belief that this is good for everyone involved. Not so in most frontier markets. Here the Zero-Sum Mindset is dominant, and people think, if I give away my knowledge, I won't be needed anymore. I won't be able to provide for my family. If I give away anything—power, food, knowledge—I lose!

In times of war and famine, this belief kept people alive. It makes complete sense to hoard everything when the supply seems exhaustible and nothing new is being created. But building a business calls for the creation of something new, and that is definitely not a zero-sum belief.

Behavior: Reluctance to celebrate the successes of others.

Zero-sum thinking rears its head when individuals try to get ahead. A person's success is generally not celebrated by those around him or her. The thinking is, "There is only so much success available (i.e., it is a zero-sum). If they get ahead, then I can't." It all adds up to a damper on individuals moving ahead of the pack with new ideas and extra effort; they get beaten down quickly.

The Zero-Sum Mindset dampens mentoring and personnel development, especially among managers, because they fear giving too much knowledge and power to those under them.

Thankfully, you can leverage three valuable and effective responses.

Response: Shift the belief, don't concentrate on the symptoms.

To shift a behavior, there must be a shift in the belief that drives that behavior. Do not concentrate on the symptoms. Hoarding and lack of collaboration are symptoms of a scarcity mindset. If the belief is that there is only one pie and it never gets bigger, bake more pies!

If the belief is that there is only
one pie and it never gets bigger,
bake more pies!

Demonstrate, highlight and reward anytime someone makes the pie get bigger.

Response: Demonstrate win-win possibilities through exercises and case studies.

You can find a number of win-win or collaboration team exercises on the Internet. Some of the best are variations of the classic Prisoners' Dilemma. This is a powerful exercise in which a collaborative win-win approach always pays the highest dividends over time.

YouTube gives you access to many visual stories of people and teams who practice win-win solutions. "The Profit" on the CNBC channel is one of my favorite TV shows because it showcases many good business principles, including win-win thinking. Marcus Lemonis, a well-known investor, finds struggling small businesses and applies good business and management principles to turn them around or take them to the next level. At the Business Innovation Hub, we watched one episode together at the end of each week and discussed what we learned.

Response: Highlight and reward win-win behavior.

To shift, individuals must prove to themselves that a certain belief (and resultant behavior) will no longer get them to their desired vision. They must adopt a stronger belief that "overrides" the zero-sum belief.

Honor and respect are two of the most valued rewards/ treasures in the world, as we have seen previously. You as a leader can slowly "de-power" the Zero-Sum Mindset if you reward win-win behavior consistently, especially if you do this by honoring those who exhibit it. The belief that an abundance mindset brings them honor, respect, power and success, overpowers the historical belief that life is zero-sum.

Make sure to highlight and explain, and then honor in public, anyone you see truly delegating power to those under him or her. Reward your employees with honor and additional information and responsibility, when you see them being generous with information or knowledge you've given them.

When someone is promoted, be sure to point out exactly why the person was promoted. Present the ways that all employees can move up, make more money, or increase their responsibilities. Then celebrate, celebrate, celebrate!

The Zero-Sum Mindset often goes hand in hand with the mindset we will look at next: **Survival Mindset.**

CHAPTER 11

SURVIVAL MINDSET

The air conditioner units at Roshan's Kabul headquarters were installed with such disdain for quality that I could scarcely believe they were still attached to the wall. Glass panes were broken and hastily patched, electrical tape hung haphazardly, and every unit was installed crookedly. I told the installer that I simply would not pay for the work.

With rising voice, the Afghan installer insisted that he had finished the work and deserved to be paid. After hours of haggling, he threatened to head off and get the police. "Look," I said, "you know we're going to be the largest mobile phone company in the country. I will give you a hundred more units to install as we expand if you do a good job installing these eight units. But if you don't fix these units, you'll never get another penny of work from us."

He snapped back without even a moment's hesitation, "No! I want my money right now!"

I could not grasp his thought process. It took me years to fully understand that, in that exchange, I had had one of my most stark encounters with the Survival Mindset pervading Afghanistan and many other frontier markets.

For the installer, guaranteeing survival for his family that day was far more sensible than gambling on a future that recent history told him was anything but certain. He had lived hand-to-mouth for twenty-three years as war raged around him, raining down up to a thousand rockets a day and snuffing out life as they did. He wanted the guarantee of bread today rather than the promise of gold tomorrow. Could I blame him? And yet I had to build a company that would last for years within this mindset.

The Survival Mindset and the Zero-Sum Mindset are the biggest impediments to progress and growth in frontier markets.

Along with the Zero-Sum Mindset, the Survival Mindset is the biggest impediment to progress and growth in conflict-affected and frontier markets[37]. This mindset weaves itself through and underpins almost every transaction and relationship. Coming to grips with the reality of the Survival Mindset, recognizing its incarnations, and working to mitigate its negative effects are essential for managing successfully in these kinds of environments.

---

37. The Inglehart-Welzel Cultural Map shows countries plotted according to Survival vs. Self-Expression values on the x-axis based on the World Values Survey of 2015 (www.worldvaluessurvey.org). Notice that those in the Survival half are generally less developed economically. "Inglehart–Welzel cultural map of the world." Wikipedia. November 9, 2017. Accessed December 12, 2017. https://en.wikipedia.org/wiki/Inglehart%E2%80%93Welzel_cultural_map_of_the_world.

The wicked irony is that the Survival Mindset works. The people you are dealing with would not be standing in front of you if they were not incredibly successful survivalists. The problem, of course, is that this hitherto successful winning strategy simply will not take them to their new vision.

UNPACKING THE SURVIVAL MINDSET

Let's unpack the three beliefs, resultant behaviors, and effective responses of the Survival Mindset.

BELIEF 1: THE FUTURE IS NOT GUARANTEED; WHAT MATTERS IS ENSURING MY (AND MY FAMILY'S) SURVIVAL TODAY.

In the West, most believe that tomorrow the sun will rise, our country will continue to exist and operate, and there will be opportunities to be seized. "There's more where that came from" is a common expression in affluent, developed countries.

We assume that our families will have food on the table and the government or some agency would be there to lend a hand if there were to be an emergency or unusual circumstance.

But what if those expectations hadn't proved true over your lifetime? What if you had seen family members die in front of your eyes? What if you and your family had gone to bed hungry more than once? Would you too look only to today? It may be hard to imagine that state of mind, but you must in order to understand the Survival Mindset.

It may seem that this mindset is only seen in poor countries, but there is a significant percentage of people even in the U.S. and Europe who wake up each morning with simple survival on their minds.

Behavior: Lack of investment in future quality.

You are likely to struggle with quality at every step in a context ruled by the Survival Mindset. Investing in quality assumes that there will be a tomorrow; quick and dirty ensures your family will eat today. There is no need to build things that last.

People living in survival mode often don't actually *see* the lack of quality. Like the skill of planning, noticing quality is a muscle that becomes atrophied from lack of use. Of course, even "seeing" it doesn't mean that people will invest in it without being forced to. We can't just say, "Build it to have quality."

I once contracted a local bricklayer to build a storage shed in the back corner of our property in Kabul. As I left for work in the morning, I hastily gave instructions that he build it parallel to the two perimeter walls that met in the corner of our property. Several hours later, I returned to inspect the work. I was startled to immediately notice that, though the wall was half way up, it was most definitely not parallel to anything else on the lot. If anything, it followed the bowed line of one of the perimeter walls.

I found my young house manager, Zabi, and lined him up with the side of the house. I then had him look toward the half-built wall. "Do you see anything unusual, Zabi?" I asked.

"No, sir!" he said with conviction.

"Look again, Zabi."

"It looks good to me, Mr. Curt." He and the bricklayer simply could not see that the wall obviously bowed away from any other line on the property.

I pointed out the problem, asking Zabi how this could have happened. "You are the house manager and should be watching that this project is done correctly. Tear the wall down and start again."

Normally an Afghan would have been aghast at such an order. "What difference does it really make if it's not aesthetically proper?" they would ask. But over the years, I had ingrained in Zabi the understanding that accepting less than the best was no way to rebuild a country, and so I wouldn't accept it in our home either.

An hour later I returned to inspect the progress and saw that the wall had been torn down and restarted correctly. And there in the middle of the yard was Zabi sitting on a chair watching intently as the bricklayer laid down each and every brick in the reconstructed wall.

"What are you doing, Zabi?"

"I'm managing the building of the wall just like you said I should," he replied proudly.

Lesson number two: Afghans are literal to the bone.

Five years later Zabi stood in front of a whole group of Afghans at my going-away party and told, with obvious pride, the story of how he had learned to pay attention to quality, a practice he has continued to apply to this day in his increasingly successful career.

When you come face-to-face with this belief and behavior, here are two specific and effective responses that I have found helpful.

Response: Paint a vision; help them see possibilities.

Countries such as Afghanistan and Nigeria are the dumping ground for cheap Chinese products. One of the subtle, but powerful signals of increasing prosperity and economic security is when people in these countries become increasingly dissatisfied with buying the cheapest quality goods on the market. When you see a future ahead, you are much more likely to value quality and are willing to pay for it.

A vision of the future is the single
most powerful tool you have to
encourage investment in quality
and future planning.

A vision of the future is the single most powerful tool you have to encourage investment in quality and future planning.

It can be exceedingly tempting to address the "symptoms" of the Survival Mindset—poor planning and quality, nepotism, failure to collaborate, etc.—without first addressing the limiting mindsets and beliefs that underpin these behaviors. Simply put, such an approach is a huge waste of energy and resources.

First, make sure your own vision is strong and clear, then discover the very personal vision of each of the entrepreneurs and employees you engage with. Working together, process the steps and changes needed to get them to that vision. This is their vision, not yours, but you can journey with them as they recognize the mindsets that need to shift in order to get to their vision.

Vision doesn't have to be some grand, utopian destination. A good vision may be to see one's children finish high school or to get a promotion. Whatever it is, it has to be about more than just surviving.

A caveat: don't make the initial visions too big. Make sure employees can find some success at reaching a vision quickly—then move on to identifying another one.

Response: Demand quality and then rigorously monitor it.

Make quality personal. Being a telecoms engineer, I understand that good mobile phone reception is highly valued by

Afghans. I used the following as an (highly simplified) example when I explained the importance of quality to Zabi in the bricklaying adventures.

An antenna technician accidently knocks the mobile phone antenna on the tower out of alignment by just one degree so the signal no longer reaches Zabi's phone. The technician's response, when asked about this, is, "It's just a tiny bit out of alignment; no big deal."

I asked Zabi how he would respond to this, and he answered with indignation. He insisted that the technician should get his tail back up the tower and adjust the antenna properly.

I then asked him, "So, why don't you build the brick wall with good alignment?"

The light bulb went on.

Getting quality will still be a struggle. Continue to demand it, even in the small things and even if your staff or the entrepreneurs you're investing in don't fully understand it or buy into it. At times it will feel onerous to have to monitor quality so closely and make them do things over and over until it is correct. But the rewards for your company (and for the country) are enormous and worth the effort.

That is one way to respond to one specific, deeply held Survival Mindset belief and the resultant behavior.

I now present two more specific beliefs, the behaviors they produce, and ways you can best respond to them.

BELIEF 2: FAILURE CAN MEAN DEATH; TAKING RISKS AND FAILING IS DEVASTATING.

Risk is relative in the West. We ask our employees to be creative and take risks, but these risks are never existential. Risk *is* existential for a person living on the edge or a person who has lived through a crisis.

In the battles that these cultures are so familiar with, a warrior who takes the risk of raising his head above the parapet in the middle of a battle is liable to have his head shot off. That same mindset seems to carry over into the way in which people act within the workplace and broader marketplace. They are reluctant to stick their head up above the parapet. They do not want to distinguish themselves by acting differently than the crowd, therefore attracting unneeded attention to themselves.

In business settings, you will see the Survival Mindset in the absolute fear of failure: failure is death! Failure is a luxury only for the rich, powerful, and secure.

This produces three predictable behaviors.

Behavior: Reluctance to try new ideas or to think outside the box.

Don't be surprised if your employees don't naturally take chances or are unwilling to try new ideas.

The Survival Mindset also breeds victimization, which, in turn, rears its ugly head in blame and shirking of responsibility. When things go bad, those living out of a Survival Mindset will tend to externalize blame, point fingers at others, and make excuses.

Now, before we judge our colleagues and clients in these environments too harshly, we should admit that we see this same Survival Mindset play out in the U.S. in the scourge of personal injury lawsuits. I put a cup of steaming hot coffee between my legs while driving and then sue McDonald's when it spills and I burn my nether regions. I play the victim and blame everyone else except me.

People in post-conflict or post-dictatorship countries such as Afghanistan, Nigeria, or Myanmar (Burma) have far, far more excuses to have developed the Survival Mindset than we have. In both places, however, the truth remains that a reluctance to take responsibility will create a very real obstacle to progress.

BEHAVIOR: WEAK PLANNING AND STRATEGIZING SKILLS.

People with a Survival Mindset tend to be very poor future strategic planners. Opportunities to exercise this skill have been very limited in a context of sustained conflict, chronic poverty, or dictatorial political leadership.

Strategic thinking implies forward thinking and the ability to predict, with some reasonable accuracy, what the future is likely to offer. But why plan for tomorrow if it is not probable?

These behaviors call for two decisive and effective responses.

Response: Reward risk and innovation quickly.

The belief that risk has no reward must be fundamentally shifted. The only effective way to shift this belief is to reward risk and celebrate failure.

I talked about this in the section "Unpacking Inside-the-Box Thinking" on page 122, but it bears repeating. You must reward any kind of risk-taking quickly. Think of your staff's and your investees' risk horizon as being only one day ahead. That's what war, trauma, and poverty do to you. The only way you will push that risk horizon further out is by rewarding what short-term risk they will take. Short-term risk, quick reward. Innovative idea, quick reward. You don't even need to wait to see if it works or not.

Response: Set short-term goals with rewards, then slowly add longer-term goals.

Set short-term goals and reward reaching those goals. By short term, I mean any goals that are longer than tomorrow. Really! Don't set up long-term performance goals; they're essentially useless. Reward immediately, then begin stretching the timeline out as you see the mindset begin to switch.

Initially the Survival Mindset must be acknowledged and worked with. Don't punish those in survival mode who ask to be paid or rewarded immediately. Slowly increase the horizon as trust is built and the benefits of longer-term thinking are taught and demonstrated.

More than anything, just practice. The more you go through the strategic planning process and demonstrate the successes and rewards of planning, the more those with the Survival Mindset will gather evidence that allows them to shift their belief. Success is reached when they initiate and use the planning themselves.

BELIEF 3: I CANNOT TRUST OTHERS OUTSIDE MY FAMILY, CLAN, OR GROUP.

In war and crisis, you learn to trust only your relatives—your family and clan. Not too many years ago this was true in the U.S., too; the Italians, Irish, and Jews in New York fought each other and wouldn't think of trusting each other, much less intermarrying. Whites against blacks, Northerners against Southerners—the U.S. history is replete with ethnocentricity.

Even now we see that when a population feels threatened, it starts to become suspicious of "others." The ethnic and family fault lines reappear.

When you grow up in this environment, you learn very early on, "Don't trust outsiders!"

INVESTOR TIP

As an investor, you will find that frontier markets are rife with distrust and the ethnocentricity that ensues. But you can take great satisfaction in the fact that one of the main antidotes to ethnocentricity is economic prosperity and having common frontiers to tame. Your creation of jobs and the example you set in creating a fair and diverse workplace is medicine against ethnocentricity.

Behavior: Nepotism and ethnocentricity thrive.

The belief that trust is best reserved for members of one's family, clan, or tribe contributes to a significant problem of nepotism, favoritism, and ethnocentricity. The entrepreneurs you invest in and your staff will tend to hire their relatives and clan members or shift contracts to family or tribal members. As an outsider, it can be extremely difficult to recognize this when it happens. This is particularly difficult because family networks are often more far reaching than the typical nuclear family unit in the West. A third cousin once removed is considered "close" family, while in the West we would not have the faintest idea who this would be.

You can't sit this one out. Instead, you need to take decisive action.

Behavior: Weak collaboration.

I talked about weak collaboration as a consequence of the Zero-Sum Mindset and I must mention it again here.

Collaboration requires a win-win mindset that is missing in a zero-sum view of life. It also needs a measure of trust that is often missing in the Survival Mindset.

Response: Make a strict rule that one family member cannot work under another family member.

Recognize the immense pressure your employees feel from their families to get further family members hired at the company. Make the rule that multiple family members can work at your company, but they cannot be in the same reporting line. Then create a clear and transparent hiring process where family relationships are made public. Make sure that one family member is never involved in the decision to hire another family member.

My strong suggestion is that you, as the expat, are involved in final approval on all hires in the early stages of a company. This may seem daunting and paternalistic, but the family and clan pressure over time has a way of wearing down even the best employees. They need a "cover," ("It wasn't my decision") to give to their family to protect their own honor. (See my story about Ali back at the beginning of Chapter 5: Relationships: Community vs. Individual.)

Response: Put in place simple, but comprehensive, systems for approvals and monitoring of contracts.

My maxim is KISS KIT: Keep It Simple, Stupid (KISS) and Keep It Transparent (KIT).

Keep in mind all of the beliefs we have been learning when you design the system. Test every step against those beliefs.

Imagine that the beliefs bring the default behaviors; create a system that encourages the positive behaviors and mitigates the negatives.

Remember this: Contracts equal money and money equals survival. Contracts can easily become a way to guide work to relatives and community members or they can become a way to get kickbacks which go toward supporting your family and community.

Don't get judgmental here. Chances are good that you would bend the rules too if you were in the same position. Instead, think logically, think cunningly, but, for heaven's sake, keep it simple. Let common sense reign.

A whole book could be written on creating contracting systems that work within various cultures, but here are the four most important things to remember:

1. *Let your national colleagues help you design the system.* Remember that you, as a foreigner, will never be able to see fully behind the veil.
2. *Ensure that contract systems are practical and efficient.* If they are not, they become burdensome and therefore not adopted—with conviction and ownership—as a positive tool of the business. It is almost as if the system itself becomes a kind of enemy to be fought against and exploited.
3. *Practice transparency by laying out every single (simple) step for all to see.* The public aspect of the system helps to keep people more honest.
4. *Keep it simple.* The more complex the system is, the more loopholes there will be to exploit.

Here's an example of exploiting loopholes. As we were installing the Roshan mobile phone system across Afghanistan, we decided, due to technical issues unique to the country, to change the delay between a connection being made and the moment the call started charging the customer. The delay had been one second previously; we changed it to three seconds.

We told no one, but within days we suddenly discovered that the system was being flooded with three-second phone calls. These were, of course, not generating any revenue for us. The clever users had discovered that they could make numerous calls at no cost.

The conversations were obviously very chunky: "Hello, this is Ehsan ..." hang up. "Let's meet at Hazara Yak Shab restaurant ..." hang up, and on and on. The knowledge of this change had spread like wildfire across Afghanistan within days and made a dent in our revenue until we changed it back.

Think through the culture and mindsets that are present in your business and in the country.

If it is an Honor/Shame culture, then make the contracting and financial processes public for a better chance at keeping people honest. If it is a Power/Fear culture, put extra teeth behind it, especially the loss of position or demotion, and be absolutely sure that every violation is punished (a good reason for keeping the rules simple and enforceable).

Where a Survival Mindset is evident, be sure to create a general environment of abundance and generosity in your organization. Then make contracting and financial accounting so tight that it is simply not seen as a potential place to find money. Remember that tight doesn't mean complex. Tight means as few variables and ambiguities as possible.

—§—

Now that we have explored the very powerful Survival Mind-set, we will look at one final mindset that is closely related: **Limited Possibilities.**

CHAPTER 12
LIMITED POSSIBILITIES MINDSET

Without exception, people look at the range of options in front of them and choose the one they think is best for themselves and their community. The ability to open up new options and new possibilities to your clients, colleagues, or employees will be your single most powerful weapon against what may seem in the moment to be irrational or corrupt choices.

People look at the range of
options in front of them and
choose the one they think is best
for themselves and
their community.

The key is *not* to say, "Don't choose bad options" when people are making poor choices. Instead, do all you can to increase the number of good options they are able to perceive. People will choose a better option, if better possibilities are added to the array they see in front of them.

UNPACKING THE LIMITED POSSIBILITIES MINDSET

Let's unpack this issue as it's related to corruption, especially in the business arena. Corruption is without question one of the biggest brakes on economic success and therefore on the success of any investments in frontier and emerging markets.

BELIEF 1: CORRUPTION IN ALL ITS FORMS IS AN INEVITABLE AND UNAVOIDABLE PART OF LIFE.

The only way to succeed in business is to give and take bribes and "play the game" in whatever way is necessary to survive.

It took me one month, seventy-two signatures, and twenty-seven letters to get approval from the Afghan government to sign a lease for a 33 foot by 40 foot (10 meters by 12 meters) plot of land for one of our first cell phone towers. For a $100 bribe, however, I could have had the lease approved and signed by the Afghan government office in an hour.

Welcome to the wonderful world of *baksheesh*—"gifts"—and bribes.

Corruption works for the individuals taking the bribes. Of course, study after study shows that increasing corruption correlates to increasing poverty and decreasing human development. But corruption is often *the* most sensible and effective strategy that a person sees in a context, where the Survival

Mindset is strong, resources scarce, and the future bleak. For such a person, corruption works at the most basic and immediate level.

Why wouldn't someone try to get as much money as possible *today*, no matter what the law says? I'm not excusing corruption or the taking of bribes. However, telling a starving person, "Don't steal food," is rarely going to have the effect you want.

Jean Jobs, an experienced international leadership trainer and founder of YellowMarker[38], an innovative training and consulting company, is right on the mark: "Most individuals who participate in corruption do not identify their actions as corrupt. They have reasonable motivations and values being served by those actions. In their view of their current situation, choosing corruption makes perfect sense and they will continue to make the same choice day after day, unless presented with another, better option."

In its essence, a person with this perspective believes there is "only one truth" and only one possibility in the situation and acts accordingly.

This Limited Possibilities Mindset is a very human mindset. It is exacerbated by an environment where many possibilities are, in fact, limited because of real lack of peace, lack of resources, lack of education, etc. It is often woven into the mindsets of Zero-Sum and Survival.

Behavior: Regulatory, contract, and internal corruption is found at every step of doing business.

There are three types of business corruption you will most often encounter in frontier markets. First is what I would call "regulatory" corruption. This almost always comes from a gov-

---

38. www.yellowmarker.com

ernment entity, but can come from other regulatory bodies which create market rules and regulations. The second is contract corruption. It is corruption involved in winning contracts. The third is internal corruption. This ranges from how a company's subcontracts are awarded all the way to simple internal financial fraud.

Let's look at how to deal creatively and humbly with corruption among government and regulatory officials as this is the biggest existential threat to investments in frontier markets.

EFFECTIVE RESPONSES

"It is impossible to do business in frontier and emerging markets without paying bribes."

That is what many people will tell you, but I am here to tell you that we proved them *wrong*. Though it may be the hardest issue you will face in your business, it is possible to stay clean.

Before we go another step, we need to acknowledge that we in the West have our own insidious forms of corruption. Politicians in the U.S. raise huge amounts of legal money from corporations and interest groups who have beneficial legislation in front of their committees. It is not illegal, but most neutral observers would say it benefits the "payers" at the expense of everyone else. How is that not corruption? Foreign aid money from Europe and North America goes to the same implementing organizations over and over even though a neutral observer would often conclude that the results are dismal. How is that, at its essence, not corruption?

It is time we stopped telling people *not* to be corrupt. Instead, we need more effective strategies for limiting corruption by opening up the possibilities available to people. Simply telling people "Don't be corrupt!" fails to address the core mindsets that drive these decisions.

Don't tell them, "Don't be corrupt"; work on increasing the possibilities in frontier and emerging markets rather than lecturing people on making bad choices.

It is time to work on increasing the possibilities in frontier and emerging markets rather than lecturing people on making bad choices.

Response: Enroll people in a vision that opens up possibilities.

There is no more powerful antidote against systemic corruption than vision. Without vision, there is no appetite for something different. Our success at Roshan came in part because we enrolled people, especially government officials, in a vision for creating a world-class mobile phone system in which they played an important part.

A person who sees another possible way to survive, will almost always choose against corruption, especially in a country where the majority religion condemns corruption. You can appeal to values, but if aligning with values means their family doesn't have food on the table, can you blame them for picking corruption? Open up possibilities. Reward those who deal with you honestly; with money or gifts if you are allowed, but most importantly, with large doses of honor and respect.

Response: Build and maintain relationships, especially in the hierarchy above the person who is demanding the bribes.

Most government officials and businesspeople in frontier markets are torn between what seems like a choice between survival and honesty in their dealings with you. Much of what will determine which side they fall is their relationship with you.

If you show them respect and maintain that you simply won't pay bribes, you often will be able to find a way forward, even though the effort may be arduous as I describe in my story above.

People are far more likely to look actively for other ways to fill their immediate needs than to engage in bribery or other forms of corruption, if they have a relationship with you.

Response: Be creative.

A commander in Afghanistan wanted Roshan to pay him a cash bribe in exchange for approval to put up mobile phone antennas. We refused to do it and instead came up with a creative (and ethical) alternative to a payoff. We had already budgeted to put in some children's playgrounds in his region. We told him that we would not put cash in his hand, but we would give him all the credit for bringing a children's playground to his people. He agreed and a few months later, he cut the ribbon at the opening of the park and gained great honor in his community.

There are often creative ways of navigating around corruption, particularly bribes, if you know the culture. They might include alternative rewards or playing the shame game of "I'm a guest and you're treating me poorly." Sometimes even use the ignorant foreigner excuse: "What? I don't know what you're asking of me. "

Consult your colleagues and local friends if you don't know the culture well enough. Very often they will have already discovered creative methods of their own to get around payments.

BRIBES VS. FACILITATING PAYMENTS

What is the difference between a bribe and a "facilitating payment"? Can you pay someone to put your paper at the top of the stack, an action that is not illegal, but is preferential? Does that make a difference if you know that money is going straight into their pocket?

My policy has been: If they will give me an official receipt, I'll consider paying a "fee" in order to get things done more quickly. What happens, though, if you're being essentially blackmailed by a government official who creates a rule that he says you've broken and asks for a "penalty?" For $1,000, it will all go away, but you know it never should have been there to begin with.

At other times, you may need to pay a "facilitator"—someone who has valuable relationships that you do not, who can get things done for you. Customs clearance is one example; we couldn't navigate this complex system ourselves, so we hired a clearance agent who facilitated our application. We made sure that everything we were asking for was legal and left it to the facilitator to get it done.

Response: If all else fails, use power and fear.

There are times you will need to use power and fear. Even if it is never used, this power and fear has to be set up from the very start of the relationship with the official. Every society will have subtly different ways of communicating power and position—body language and name-dropping are almost universal. Cultivate your understanding of these dynamics. Acknowledge their power, but make sure they also are left with no doubt about your own power. A good deputy will navigate the subtleties of this balance deftly.

If you are stuck, work your way up the power chain, again respectfully. In almost all cases, I advise against publicly shaming the one asking for a bribe. Often you will find that somewhere up the chain is a person who will clear the path just because she can. She will help because she gets your honor and your recognition of her power and that is worth more than money to her. (A caveat: there is an expectation of a returned favor down the line. Be prepared to creatively "reward" her in some non-corrupt way.)

*Response: Finally, **don't** pay bribes!*

The moment you pay a bribe, you have opened the gate, and the horses won't return to the barn. As the Bedouins would say, you let the camel's nose in the tent. It takes a lot of conviction and strength to stand against what seems like impossibility. Create a vision to guide you through the labyrinth.

If you're only about making money and think there is nothing inherently wrong with paying bribes to get your way—put this book down now. This is not for you. Corruption ultimately cannot lead to progress. Leaders need to have courage and make tough decisions that may prolong some difficulties, but are worth it in the end.

BELIEF 2: THE ONLY CHOICES I HAVE FOR ANY DECISION ARE THE ONES I SEE IMMEDIATELY IN FRONT OF ME.

In frontier markets, people have come to believe that the choices they have are only those that are immediately obvious.

In general, the poorer the country and the worse its education system, the more you will see the Limited Possibilities Mindset. And note, this mindset contains the threads of the Survival and Zero-Sum Mindsets as well.

Behavior: What seem like obvious possible choices are missed.

This can be baffling to outsiders. Your investees and employees will at times simply not see alternate possibilities when confronted with a choice, be it personal or business. What seems obvious to you never crosses their minds.

In business, this can be highly limiting and detrimental. It's related to the lack of creativity and inside-the-box thinking that is common in frontier markets.

I'm writing this chapter in Nigeria, where I've been Skyping with one of my former Afghan employees. He is desperately looking for a job in a stagnant economy. He's been offered a job that includes driving and selling, but he won't take it because the salary is too small to support his family. The business is a startup, so it can't pay the salary he's demanding. In his mind it was end of story, end of opportunity. The only choices he sees are to take the job and not make enough or turn down the job. Are there no other possible ways to get paid adequately, I ask? None, he says.

Many of you reading this see the obvious possibility: commissions. Why not take a salary for the driving and ask for a commission for the selling? This hadn't crossed his mind. The reality is that commissions are not common in Afghanistan, partly because there is inherent risk implied and that risk is not worth it when you're making just enough to feed your family. But this acquaintance did not even see the possibility of commissions in front of him, so he was choosing between the only two possibilities he did see.

This scenario is played out over and over again in frontier markets. How do you shift it?

Response: Open up possibilities.

As we've seen, the most powerful antidote to limited possibilities is vision. Those with limited possibilities are like men and women walking with their eyes on their feet. Vision lifts up the eyes to see new and better ways to travel. It creates a map for moving into a new future.

Having a vision forces one to look at multiple ways to get to it. A rock climber whose vision is to reach the top of a shear wall studies the possible routes before embarking. She then deals with the dead ends that she couldn't see from the bottom by readjusting her route accordingly. All possible new routes are analyzed with the vision in mind of reaching the top.

"Heroes are not the product of great societies. Heroes are the cause of great societies."—Roy H. Williams[39]

Tell me who your heroes are and I will tell you what you value and what are your priorities. Tell me who a country's heroes are and I will tell you where they're headed, especially economically.

Ask an American who their heroes are and, among others, you will usually hear the name Steve Jobs, Oprah, Mark Zuckerberg, Sheryl Sandberg, or even Beyoncé—all successful entrepreneurs.

I've asked groups of new-generation Afghans over the years to list off their heroes. In the early years after the Taliban were run out, they would literally sit there and look at me as if they didn't understand. Finally, someone would venture to name a historical king or perhaps the Afghan Joan of Arc, Malalai of Maiwand. In later years, they might mention a newly ascendant cricket or soccer (i.e., football) player, or maybe a singer, or poet. Not once in all the years of asking did they ever mention an entrepreneur or businessperson. Is it any wonder that the Afghan economy creates almost nothing of long-term value?

Heroes demonstrate possibilities. Heroes have the power to transform a country. When you highlight and celebrate local heroes, whether in business or in other endeavors, you prove to your investees, entrepreneurs, and employees that despite all the obstacles, success is possible. Find these heroes, cultivate them, and watch them open up possibilities to their peers.

It's time for impact and social investors to intentionally find and invest in the entrepreneurs in frontier markets who will become the heroes that set the tone for the whole economy. They are there. Do good while doing well.

Response: Challenge decisions and demand justifications.

Challenge the decision maker to justify their choice even on simple decisions. Make sure they have exhausted all possible choices before making their decision. Sometimes it is as simple as asking "what is another possibility here?"

Group brainstorming may be needed to dislodge new possibilities. Use brainstorming often so the brain muscle gets exercised and possibility thinking becomes the norm (see page 90 and 136 for brainstorming ideas).

Response: Reward those who make good and creative choices in the workplace.

I have talked throughout the book about the power of reward. Dig for the ways in which your investees, employees, and peers receive reward most powerfully. Look at the ways the culture rewards people. Remember that in many of the countries you work, public honor is right at the top of the list. Then reward in these ways those who practice possibility thinking.

Response: Use a reminder prop that reminds your staff and entrepreneurs to look at things in a new way.

As I described earlier, in Afghanistan we used a sheet of paper that was blank on one side and had a picture or writing on the other side to illustrate that there was always more than one way to look at a "truth." We actually went so far as to laminate a small 6 centimeter by 10 centimeter card with a picture on one side and blank on the other, and gave it to each person. Whenever we sensed someone—or the group itself—was getting into narrow and inside-the-box thinking, we could hold up the

---

39. Quoted from a conversation with Roy H. Williams during marketing training at the Wizard Academy in Austin, Texas, on January 3, 2010.

card or reference it. It reminded people to think about what might be on the other side of the "truth" they were stuck on at the moment. Simple, but powerful.

LIMITED POSSIBILITIES MINDSET: PERCEPTION IS REALITY

Finally, let's deal with one of the unique consequences of the Limited Possibilities Mindset: perception is reality. Logic, facts, and reason don't always overcome "the way it looks."

Not too many centuries ago the Western world believed the sun revolved around the earth. We perceived the sun rising in the east and setting in the west. So, it must be true. Science and education later informed us that there was a much bigger picture beyond our earthly perceptions.

Perceptions or simple facts without context get blown up into strange conspiracies or exaggerated narratives in countries where the education system is lacking, and sources of information are limited. I witnessed this firsthand in Roshan, on a day when a flood of customers came into our office. All of their phones were off and their perplexed and concerned looks communicated fear.

"Will the viruses kill us?" the customers asked me.

My mind raced to understand if they somehow thought I was a doctor.

"What viruses?"

"The viruses that come from the phone," they responded.

They explained to me, "Everyone in the city is turning off their phone because we heard that a phone virus is going around. It jumps from the phone to your ear and destroys your brain. If you answer a call from a certain number, you will die."

Talk about viral marketing—in reverse! Within hours, thanks to the powerful chain of relational connections that crisscrosses most frontier and emerging countries, the rumor that a deadly virus was afoot had spread across Afghanistan. We were losing thousands of dollars an hour. Quickly we put out press releases and created a script for our customer-facing employees to quell the crisis. The same way it reared up, it settled down: word of mouth.

When perception becomes reality without facts and logic to back it up, the choices that are perceived to be available are very often faulty and almost always very limited.

Challenge this kind of thinking. Explore the idea by asking them questions instead of laughing and shaming them. Encourage people to show evidence for their perceptions, then challenge the evidence. It can be tiring, but it is worth it as you see your employees begin to reject unsubstantiated stories and make informed business and life choices.

SUMMARY

We have now covered three worldviews;

- Honor/Shame
- Power/Fear
- Innocence/Guilt

Each of these worldviews is a bundle of cultural dimensions, five of which we explored:

- Relationships: Community vs. Individual
- Power Distance: High vs. Low
- Communication: Direct vs. Indirect
- Productivity: People vs. Tasks and Time
- Destiny: Fatalism vs. Personal Control

Overlaying culture are mindsets born from experiences, often traumatic. We looked at three:

- Zero-Sum
- Survival
- Limited Possibilities

At their core, every one of these worldviews, cultural dimensions, and mindsets is a belief or a bundle of beliefs and every belief drives behaviors and actions.

Every human BEHAVIOR comes out of a core BELIEF.

If you look at every cultural encounter through the lens of the Belief Tool, you will be prepared to interpret the actions and behaviors in ways that bring the results you desire.

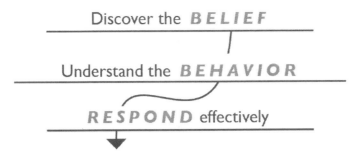

Discover the *BELIEF*

Understand the *BEHAVIOR*

RESPOND effectively

And finally, without exception, people make the best choice among the possibilities they see before them. If you help open up possibilities and enroll them in a vision, your investees, the entrepreneurs you coach, and your staff will make the choices that bring them closer to their vision and you closer to yours.

CONCLUSION

A decade after that fateful afternoon spent negotiating mobile phone access with twelve elders in a dusty room in Afghanistan's deep south, Destageer and I again found ourselves at the negotiating table.

Afghanistan had transformed in that decade. The mudbrick walls and worn carpet of our first tribal meeting were now replaced by a state-of-the-art facility at the American University, where we were building the country's first business accelerator. The bearded and turbaned elders were replaced by the owners of a commercial tailoring company employing 200 tailors, including seventy mostly uneducated women who were being given a life-changing skill.

Market towns that had been flattened were now teeming with business. Streets on which women had rarely been seen were now filled with the eager chattering of girls returning home from school. In almost every Afghan's hand was a mobile phone from which they could connect to the information superhighway.

Of course, forward movement had not been felt by the country across the board and in some areas it seemed the hope of the early years was receding, but there was no doubt that broad economic progress had been attained.

Together, Destageer and I had helped to build a $1 billion telecoms company at a time when Afghanistan had little physical or human capital from which to build. Make no mistake; frontier market entrepreneurship is not for the fainthearted! Success had required an almost foolhardy vision backed up with a serious injection of capital. It had also required a level of cultural intelligence that few of us from the outside world could have anticipated needing.

Frontier market entrepreneurship
is not for the fainthearted! Success
requires deep
inter-cultural intelligence.

What I learned about beliefs and behaviors in this frontier market helped our company succeed in Afghanistan. At the end of the day, though, it all comes down to people. And to this day, Destageer remains the single greatest asset to my success in business and in life in Afghanistan.

Destageer intimidated me when we first met at the Kabul InterContinental Hotel. This towering man with broad shoulders carried the proud tradition of a fierce Pashtun warrior in his face. As I listened to him speak, any sense of intimidation was quickly replaced by the unmistakable conviction that I had found my deputy. Here was a man of evident intelligence, but also of strength, integrity, and a kind of dignity that belied his years.

As I dealt with contractors, commanders, warlords, and government officials—sometimes all wrapped in the same person—Destageer acted both as my deputy and as my translator. Initially, as Destageer learned the mobile phone business, he translated my instructions word for word. Very quickly, my trust increased and I told him he had my permission to not even use my words if he felt I was going down the wrong path or if I was in danger of making a major cultural gaffe. My only request was that he let me know, then or later, what "I" had said.

Over my fourteen years in Afghanistan, Destageer became my cultural interpreter. He helped me bore down to the core of the Belief Tool and unmask the reason for the behaviors and decisions that I saw around me. He helped me shift in my understanding of how to be successful in frontier markets.

At the same time, Destageer honestly and openly looked at his own mindsets forged out of years of surviving Soviet gunship attacks, Taliban chicanery, hunger, and bitterly cold days. Where these mindsets limited his progress toward his vision, he shifted. As Destageer shifted and learned, I did as well. And in that mutual shifting and learning, a picture emerged of exactly what it takes to succeed in frontier markets—East and West coming together to join strengths and make a difference.

In my final year working with Destageer at Roshan, I encouraged him to increasingly step into my role. I became the figurehead boss who lent his foreign credentials to Destageer, and then I sat back as Destageer took over the show. I made sure that any official we met knew that Destageer spoke for me and that any promise he made was a promise from me and from the rest of the company. When I left Roshan, Destageer took over my job. It was one of my proudest days.

Destageer's success is also the story of the extraordinary and untapped possibility that lies in frontier markets. Today, a man who trained as a nurse with the Red Cross (ICRC) is the chief sales officer for Roshan, a billion-dollar company.

If I can leave you with one final lesson as you begin your own journey into frontier markets, it would be this: find your own Destageer. If chosen wisely, your deputy will be your greatest asset for navigating the cultural minefield effectively.

Turning over the Business Innovation Hub to Destageer (by Curt Laird)

YOUR OWN
JOURNEY

There are boundless investment and business opportunities in frontier markets. Very few have the courage to venture in. If you are one of those very few, join me on the journey.

The risks are many, but the rewards are worth it, not only in profit, but also in personal satisfaction and fulfillment. I have been profoundly changed for the better from my time in frontier markets. Entrepreneurs in these markets yearn for outside investors to come in and partner with them. You get to do what you love as well as contribute to the success of a country and people—making a profit while doing good.

I have now set the foundations of the inter-cultural intelligence required to invest in and grow businesses in frontier markets. I hope this book helps you take the first step toward navigating the cultural minefields you will find. I encourage you to read and share it with your colleagues and partners.

Beyond that, I invite you to continue the conversation with me. If you are a social or impact investor, or your company needs consulting in cross-cultural entrepreneurship and international management, please write to:

curt@theculturekey.com.

I look forward to hearing from you.

ACKNOWLEDGMENTS

My parents birthed me in a foreign land and gave me the privilege of growing up in multiple countries each with a multitude of cultures. More importantly, they gave me a love for humanity and modeled a life of serving others. Thank you, Dad and Mom! You are my heroes.

I traveled the world in my single days always with my eyes open for a soulmate and journey-mate who had a vision of her own for the hard places and a love of people. It took forty-nine years (okay, I guess I didn't start looking as a toddler) and a lengthy stay in Afghanistan to find **the one I'd been looking for all that time. Katrina,** you are perfect for me. We have just enough cultural similarities—being third-culture kids—and just enough shared experiences—having grown up on opposite sides of the same island, New Guinea—to complement our cultural differences and make a powerful and enriching mix. You are woven throughout this book as you spent countless hours reading, reorganizing, editing, and essentially co-authoring it. I love you!

When I was ten, I met a Greek boy in **the jungles of Papua who would become my soulmate. Johnathan Macris** embodies deep, deep integrity and faith mixed with endless words of encouragement and genuine, loyal, loving friendship. He prayed fervently that I would find my "Katrina" as he had found his Miriam and had so much faith that he gave me a wedding gift twenty years before I married her. You are a powerful example to me, Johnathan.

In 2003, I met **my Afghan brother, Destageer.** Much of this book has Destageer woven through it as we learned how to bridge the East/West, Muslim/Christian, and Afghan/American divide and build multiple businesses at the same time. I owe 90 percent of my success in Afghanistan to this gentle, wise, visionary man of integrity who guided me through the minefields, both real and figurative. In the process we became brothers, proving that any divide can actually become a bond where there is love. It's been a joy to travel with you all these years, Destageer.

Without each of you, there would be no book to share with the world.

My Top Crowdfunding Contributors (my long-suffering supporters who gave money toward this project more than five years ago and are just now getting their reward!)—Henrik Enell, Curt and Cari Dahl, Iain W. Aitken and Riitta-Liisa Kolehmainen-Aitken, Glen and Vida Laird, Jonathan and Cindee Raney, Marta Rivera Long, Meredith Leal, Jeff Quinlan, Leon Nyachae, Amy Meredith, Anonymous Texan, Zack and Cindy Taylor, John and Erin McSwain, Jonathan Nicoli, Jim and Carolyn Hively, Floyd and Mary Laird, Chris Clements, Mark Jones, Brian Arthur Frederick, Anonymous Irian Jaya MK, Sparkie Bethel and Renuka George, Andrew Fletcher, Sean Chandler, Marchien Niemeijer, RJ Blank, Walter and Hilje Greenwood, Nico and Bee Bougas, Zach and Heidi Anderson, Kimberley Clark Kartchner, Dennis and Nancy Stuessi, Douglas and Andrea Holtan, Julie Stalzer, Markus Lalla, Gus and Glenna Arnold, Eric J Popowski, Glenn Du Pree, Tiffany Young, Dan and Susan Obenschain, Gary

Bollier, Amy Lewis, Tracee Rudd, Becky Scoon, Jose and Dorrena Ortega, Jeremy Bartholomew, Anonymous Roshan colleague, Natasha Lutes, and to the 30 others who gave. You have definitely earned the rewards that you will receive.

Iain W. Aitken and Riitta-Liisa Kolehmainen-Aitken—a very special thanks to my father- and mother-in-law, first, for raising Katrina and, second, for the deep love they showed me by spending hours and hours reviewing my book. I had told them that the more red ink I saw, the more I would know they loved me. They love me a lot! Harvard-educated public health doctors, they bring a rigor to reviewing that comes from years and years of experience. Riitta-Liisa, in particular, astounds me as she corrected dozens of my grammar mistakes even though her native language is Finnish. I love you two!

Susan Ryan and Jean Jobs—you two have molded me in so many good ways, both in business and in friendship. You are almost co-authors of this book.

Jeff Quinlan—my deep, loyal, no BS friend who helped launch me on this adventure of entrepreneurship and keeps me grounded and real in so many ways.

David Sanford and Natalie Horbachevsky—behind every great book are great editors. David, you challenged me to keep my eyes on the bigger vision and to craft the book accordingly. This book has your values and heart woven throughout. Natalie, you brought it over the finish line with an experienced hand of professionalism and class.

Marco Blankenburgh—I owe so many of the foundational concepts of this book to your work and heart. You're making the world a better place.

Michelle Morgan—you believed strongly in Susan and me when we launched our training company and supported us every step of the way. That support ultimately made this book possible.

Todd and Josette McMichael—you were there from my very first days in Afghanistan in 2002. You have been those steady friends who journeyed beside me and Katrina through all the challenges of living in that majestic, mystical country.

John Hazlett and Ed "Pappy" Miner—teachers can make or break a kid. You both believed in me in such simple, but profound ways that you launched me into a life of entrepreneurship and adventure.

Zabihullah Samadi Safi—loyal friend, strong integrity, teachable, with a very bright future. I hope one day to be at the ceremony when you become minister of interior for Afghanistan.

Fawad Samadi Safi—faithful and hardworking, a man who would defend me and my family with his life.

The Ghulam Nabi Safi family—our Afghan father and mother, sisters and brothers, and family. We love you all. Thank you for taking us in as your own.

Ehssanullah Saeedi—my Kandahari brother who is a gentle Pashtun warrior for change.

The Herat Roshan Team (too many to number, but you know who you are)—together we built the best mobile phone system in all of Roshan and all of Afghanistan.

The original Roshan Regional Team (Destageer, Ezatullah, Ahmad Shah, Ehsan Ehrari, Seir Brandon, Mhmd. Asif, Max, and Aziza)—from every region of Afghanistan, you showed me the excellence of Afghan talent and taught me so many things about the rich Afghan culture.

The SRS team (again, too many to number)—we built something great and we can be very proud of the impact we had.

The Biz Hub Team (Abdullah, Arzoo, Edriss, Farahnaz, Mansoor, Mujeeb, Munib, Nabil, Rahim, Saddiq, Sayed Qavi, Shaista, Shamim, Shekib, Sher Khan, Tamana A., Tamana M.,

Todd, Rouzbeh, Wais, Zabi, Zaiba, and an unnamed Afghan)—we showed that we could build Afghan businesses. If this team was in charge of commerce for Afghanistan, the country would become the successful, progressive country they long for it to be.

Reviewers (my discerning friends and colleagues who could see the gem beneath the mud and showed me how to wash away the mud)—Iain W. Aitken and Riitta-Liisa Kolehmainen-Aitken, Vida Laird, Brian Ross, Todd and Josette McMichael, Grace How, Jean Jobs, Martha Neu, Russell Hildebrand, Beth Yoder, Evan Burns and Destageer.

Elisa Raney—a special reviewer callout to my niece who traveled to Afghanistan during the time that I was writing this book to visit my family, and who stayed up many late nights after long days at work providing millennial, Third Culture Kid, social development feedback on my book. Never forget to negotiate from strength and stand up for yourself. And don't forget that international business done right can be a powerful tool for development.

BIBLIOGRAPHY

"Adapting design, adapting programming." ODI. Accessed December 12, 2017. https://www.odi.org/events/4146-adapting-design-adapting-programming.

"Compare countries." Hofstede Insights. Accessed December 12, 2017. https://geert-hofstede.com/countries.html.

"Honor." Honor - Definition for English-Language Learners from Merriam-Webster's Learner's Dictionary. Accessed December 12, 2017. http://www.learnersdictionary.com/definition/honor.

"Inglehart–Welzel cultural map of the world." Wikipedia. November 9, 2017. Accessed December 12, 2017. https://en.wikipedia.org/wiki/Inglehart%E2%80%93Welzel_cultural_map_of_the_world.

"State of the Global Workplace: Employee Engagement Insights for the Business Leaders Worldwide (2013)", page 7, http://www.gallup.com/services/178517/state-global-workplace.aspx

"World Values Survey". WVS Database. Accessed December 12, 2017. http://www.worldvaluessurvey.org/WVSOnline.jsp.

Benedict, Ruth. *The Chrysanthemum and the Sword: Patterns of Japanese Culture*. Houghton Mifflin Harcourt, 1946.

Bennett, Ty. "The True Definition of Belief." Ty Bennett. August 4, 2009. Accessed December 12, 2017. http://tybennett.com/the-true-definition-of-belief/.

Birrane, Alison. "Yes, you should tell everyone about your failures." BBC Capital. March 13, 2017. Accessed December 12, 2017. http://www.bbc.com/capital/story/20170312-yes-you-should-tell-everyone-about-your-failures.

Blankenburgh, Marco. "12 Dimensions of Culture." Knowledge-Workx. Accessed December 12, 2017. http://www.knowledge-workx.com/articles/12-dimensions-of-culture.

Blankenburgh, Marco. "Inter-Cultural Intelligence." Knowledge-Workx. http://knowledgeworkx.com/framework/inter-cultural-intelligence. Accessed February 22, 2018.

Blankenburgh, Marco. "Three Colors of Worldview." Knowledge-Workx. Accessed December 12, 2017. http://www.knowledge-workx.com/articles/three-colors-of-worldview.

Blankenburgh, Marco. "The Three Colors of Worldview in Conflict Resolution". KnowledgeWorkx. Accessed December 12, 2017. http://knowledgeworkx.com/articles/global-intelligence/361/the-three-colors-of-worldview-in-conflict-resolution.

Blankenburgh, Marco. "Why we use the term 'Inter-Cultural Intelligence'". KnowledgeWorkx. Accessed December 12, 2017. http://knowledgeworkx.com/articles/global-intelligence/366/why-we-use-the-term-inter-cultural-intelligence.

Hall, Edward T. *Beyond Culture*. New York: Anchor Books, 1989.

Hall, Edward T. *The Silent Language*. Greenwich, CT: Fawcett, 1959.

Hofstede, Geert. *Culture's Consequences: Comparing Values, Behaviors, Institutions, and Organizations Across Nations (2nd ed.)*. Thousand Oaks, CA: SAGE Publications, 2001.

Hofstede, Geert; and Hofstede, Gert Jan. *Cultures and Organizations: Software of the Mind (Revised and expanded 2nd ed.).* New York: McGraw-Hill. 2005.

Juzi, Daniel. "Afghanistan: The Cultural Challenges of Understanding and Managing Aviation Safety." Master's thesis in Air Safety Management, City University, London, England, 2009

Lewis, Richard D. "Monochromatic and Polychromatic Cultures". Cross-Culture. January 21, 2013. Accessed March 27, 2018. http://blog.crossculture.com/crossculture/2013/01/monochromatic-and-polychromatic-cultures.html

Müller, Roland. *Honor and Shame: Unlocking the Door.* Philadelphia, PA: Xlibris Corp., 2000.

Ries, Eric. *The Lean Startup: How Today's Entrepreneurs Use Continuous Innovation to Create Radically Successful Businesses.* New York: Crown Business; 2011.

Ruiu, Gabriele, "The perverse effect of fatalism on entrepreneurial selection," *Economics Bulletin* 34, no. 2 (2014). 901-922

Sivers, Derek. "Fish don't know they're in the water", https://sivers.org/fish, June 19, 2011. Accessed March 27, 2018.

Smith, Peter B., Dugan, Shaun, and Trompenaars, Fons. "National Culture and the Values of Organizational Employees", *Journal of Cross-Cultural Psychology* 03; vol. 27, 2, (1996). 231-264, DOI:10.1177/0022022196272006, Posted online on July 27, 2016

Trompenaars, F., and Hampden-Turner, C. *Riding the Waves of Culture: Understanding Diversity in Global Business (3rd edition).* London: Nicholas Brealey Publishing, 2012.

Ward, Marguerite. "$100 billion later, Afghanistan is on the brink." CNBC. February 3, 2016. Accessed December 12, 2017. http://www.cnbc.com/2016/02/03/afghanistan-is-on-the-brink-after-us-invests-100-billion.html.

Würtz, E., "Intercultural Communication on Web sites: A Cross-Cultural Analysis of Web sites from High-Context Cultures and Low-Context Cultures". *Journal of Computer-Mediated Communication* 11, (2005). 274–299. doi:10.1111/j.1083-6101.2006.tb00313.x

ABOUT THE AUTHOR

Curt Laird is one of the most experienced foreign entrepreneurs in frontier markets. Having worked in over thirty countries, he spent the last fourteen years in Afghanistan, where he was a founding executive of Roshan—Afghanistan's largest mobile phone operator—launched his own fifty-employee training company, and founded the Business Innovation Hub, a business accelerator at the American University of Afghanistan. He is currently consulting for startups in Nigeria.

During his time in Afghanistan, Curt met his future wife, Katrina, a British-Finnish international development professional working on conflict and security sector reform. They have two children, Soraya Kaija and Josiah Jaya, both with four citizenships and the same peripatetic life their parents grew up experiencing.

Curt can be contacted at curt@curtlaird.com or go to his website at www.curtlaird.com.

Printed in Poland
by Amazon Fulfillment
Poland Sp. z o.o., Wrocław

52343365R00152